"With eloquence and wisdom, Tom Watts has extracted from the world's great religious and ethical teachings one simple rule, namely, that *the unity of the whole depends on the diversity of the parts.* Tom's sensible analysis is precisely what an anxious population needs to gain the character strength for survival and renewal. Those who fail to respect polarity are doomed to be crushed by it."

Peter Koestenbaum, Ph.D.
Recipient of the California Outstanding Professor Award
author of *The Inner Side of Greatness*

"It's been said that the unexamined life is not worth living and it's equally true that the unlived life is not worth examining. Tom Watts has fully lived and fully examined life, and shares his journey through his book, *Deal With the Devil, Dance With God,* He travels that familiar terrain of *perennial wisdom* with a fresh eye that sees simultaneously from multiple viewpoints, helping the reader *see differently* things they *already know.* With wit and insight, he unwraps the paradoxes of life – connection and separation, free will and determinism – and weaves it all together through the *harmony!of opposites* If you already know everything, this book is for you. It will tell you even more about what you already know."

Steve Bhaerman aka Swami Beyondananda
Cosmic Comic
author of *Spontaneous Evolution* (with Bruce Lipton)

i

"Tom Watts offers a rare understanding of the fundamental truths that underly our everyday existence: we are all part of the greater whole, but at the same time our minds fabricate a separation from the universe in order to understand both ourselves and the universe. This astounding viewpoint explains our challenges to getting along, offers wisdom on how to avoid hangups, and to fill life with joy, happiness, and understanding."

Keith Swenson
VP of Research & Development, Fujitsu America
author of *When Thinking Matters in the Workplace*

"Tom introduces us to the concept of *identifiction*, the illusion that a person's identity is nothing but the sum of one's positions and possessions. He argues that we extend beyond the confines of an illusory identity and offers strategies to break free from a limited concept of self.

He shows effectively that many of the ills of our existence can be traced backed to thinking of the world in dualistic terms: the other vs. the I, subject vs. object, Left vs. Right.

While the world view that Tom draws from his observations might not sit well with some traditional beliefs, his wisdom and insights will certainly appeal to every reader."

Mourad Cherfaoui, PhD
Software Security Professional
University Adjunct Professor

Deal With the Devil, Dance With God

Finding the Ultimate High in a Polarized World
by Seeing Self in Other

Tom Watts

Deal With the Devil, Dance With God

Published by
Purple Hills Books
San Jose, California, USA
http://purplehillsbooks.com/

ISBN: 978-0-9863387-7-9

In memory of my sister,

Carole

Without Steve Ruckman this book
would never have been written

CONTENTS

Contents

Introduction

If you have ever asked the following questions then this book is for you. Who am I? How can I be more authentic? How can I add meaning and purpose to my life? How can I be a happier person? How can I improve my relations with others?

Ethnic, political and religious sectarian polarization is tearing apart not only the fabric of society but the individuals within society. A close examination of the human condition reveals the myths that lead to the construction of barriers of separation.

In one way or another life is about either forming or breaking relationships and connections—with people, situations, and with one's own identity. In this book I explore obstacles to the formation of positive relationships, chief among them being our inability to see the other in us.

I also discuss other areas of division such as believing the myth that happiness, meaning, personal identity and even God are found by looking outside the self and dealing with a confused self-concept that tends to not only take sides, but that personally identifies with the side chosen. The search for the authentic Self will be a major concern of this book.

Constantly choosing sides results in unending conflicts between what appear to be opposites, such as good/evil, individual/society, freedom/control, liberal/conservative. The dilemma posed by conflicting values is what I call the "Polarity Paradox." The dilemma is a paradox because while poles are necessary, just as a coin must have two sides, life demands choosing one side over another.

Conflict and extremism are the consequences of dualistic thinking that totally accepts one side while rejecting the other.

Over emphasis on defending and protecting the self can be the cause of loneliness, alienation, and insignificance. On a political level, emphasizing differences causes extreme partisanship, wars, and authoritarianism.

The desire for unity can be the impetus behind the altruism of saints and can lead to feelings of tranquility and of being one with the world. But if one group tries to force beliefs on others, this desire can be perverted into imperialism and authoritarianism; unifying with one group necessarily entails excluding another.

I often use the terms "universe," "God," and "Cosmo" interchangeably. Although, at times, I sort of play with the notion of God, I don't subscribe to the Abrahamic religious belief in a personal God that rewards and punishes. If you are not particularly religious, don't be turned off by my occasional reference to God. To be clear, whether you subscribe to Western or Eastern religions, or whether you are atheist or agnostic, the truths are the same. I could just as easily substitute other terms for God, such as Ultimate Reality, truth, existence, the grand unifying field theory, organizing principle, ground of being, natural law, creative power, the infinite or connecting force. If God doesn't sit right with you, choose your own term. It is just easier for me to write God or Cosmo than it is to write "universal organizing principle." Cosmo, meaning an orderly, harmonious universe, is my preferred term.

Not that I want to discourage you from reading any further, but I believe that everyone's perspective contains an element of truth, and since perspectives are infinite, Truth and the authentic Self can never be defined nor finally revealed. In addition, the Polarity Paradox is not something that can be overcome since the human experience is defined by contrasts. Conflict-peace, laughter-sadness, joy-suffering, end-beginning—these are all part of the human experience. Absolute unity may be impossible to attain but the ongoing search and discovery for truth is the excitement of existence.

Throughout the book, for lack of a better term, I use "enlightenment" to describe a highly developed state of personal understanding, wisdom, equanimity and self-realization. I don't believe anyone on this planet can actually attain a continual, uninterrupted state of enlightenment since humankind, as the universe, God, or whatever, is involved in a continual process of change.

As a basically lazy person, I believe there are simple answers to life's greatest questions, or at least I hope there are, because I am too lazy to rewrite this whole book. You don't have to be a genius to find the answers, you need only know where to look. An honest and open look at who we are will reveal an intimate connection not only to each other but to existence itself, and these connections can lead to greater happiness, meaning and a stronger sense of Self. The Answer is found in the positive connections between the authentic Self, and the "Other," a term I use for anything outside of the authentic Self.

Sometimes truth seekers read self-help or spiritual literature with the same attitude as a person who reads an automobile manual on how to fix a car, or a cook who diligently follows every step in a Julia Child recipe. There may be only one best way to replace a head gasket, but there are many ways to get to the mountaintop. Don't get too carried away by studying the writings of others, for they describe their path, not yours. Philosophers develop philosophies that reflect who they are, not who you are. The lessons taught by all of the great spiritual masters, philosophers, and self-help gurus can be realized right here and now.

CHAPTER 1

AS ABOVE, SO BELOW

There is, by God's swift reckoning,
a universe in everything.
—A. M. Sullivan, Measurement

"As above, so below; as below, so above" is a profound yet simple truth. Discovering the truth of Self will unravel truths at other levels, for the fundamental principles of existence and the laws of the universe operate at every level; the quantum, atomic, personal, societal, and universal. At a fundamental level, the human experience is the experience of the universe. One of the themes of this book is that an exploration of how the laws of nature intersect the human world will bring a little more meaning to our brief sojourn on this planet by providing a vision of how we fit into the grand picture.

Many years ago I discovered a wonderful little book, *The Kabalian*, supposedly based on the secret Hermetic teachings of an ancient mythological Egyptian sage named Hermes Trismegistus. Whether he existed or not, the principles attributed to Hermes seem to accurately describe the way things work. Although there are seven principles, I'll refer specifically only to the Principle of Correspondence: "As above, so below; as below, so above." The Hermetic Principle of Correspondence is based on the scientific fact that the same laws of physics that operate on this planet also operate in the farthest reaches of the universe. Since everything in the universe emanates from the same source, all levels of organization must operate according to the same universal laws.

Newton's law of universal gravitation applies to an apple falling out of a tree on earth as much as it does to the stars orbiting the center of the galaxy or to the cause of our double chins. Newton's Third Law of Motion ("for every action there is an equal and opposite reaction") is similar to the biblical principle that you reap what you sow, which in turn underpins the Golden Rule ("do unto others what you would have them do unto you"). The first law of thermodynamics relating to the conservation of mass and energy works in our own daily lives on earth (there's no such thing as a free lunch) just as it does many light years distant in the Andromeda galaxy.

Principles underlying the microcosm (such as the workings of the human body) are the same as those governing the macrocosm (such as the solar system). So-called "spiritual laws" are just the laws of science described and applied in different ways. Just as spiritual truths can be discovered by studying the principles of matter and energy, scientific concepts can be learned from the spiritual masters. The principles underlying scientific laws all have their spiritual or psychological corollaries that apply to personal life. An understanding of how these laws operate at different levels can lead to the discovery of how they apply to the individual.

The universe was born out of conflict and its continued existence depends on balancing the opposing forces of expansion and contraction—the gravitational pull of dark matter against the expanding force of dark energy. The life-giving fires of the sun also depend on the balance between the force of gravity, which pulls atoms inward into fusion reactions, and tremendous outward pressure, which is the result of the energy left over from nuclear fusion forcing its way toward the star's surface. As long as both these forces are equal, the star continues to exist in a state of equilibrium and we earthlings continue to receive the life-giving warmth of the sun. Biological organisms also seek a state of dynamic equilibrium, or homeostasis, and the homeostasis of organisms contributes to the homeostasis of earth's many ecosystems.

The interaction between opposing forces finds expression in every field of human endeavor, whether business, politics, religion, sports or love making. We look inward to protecting the freedom and independence in our separation from others, yet look outward as we seek the approval of the crowd. We want to expand consciousness, to transcend human and physical limitations, even while the craving for material drags us down. The attraction and repulsion of positive and negative charges that is responsible for the formation of chemical bonds can be correlated to the uniting of the male and female in the formation of new life.

Motion is not only a defining characteristic for continuing existence in general—an absolutely still universe is a dead universe, but is also a requirement for the continuing life of the human mind and body.

"As above, so below" is a philosophical principle, but it also reflects the scientific worldview that the universe operates according to a few simple, comprehensible rules. All of the laws of nature are found in the cosmic egg, or what cosmologists refer to as the point of singularity before the Big Bang.

I am not making an argument for reductionism. Although the universe obeys and operates according to a few simple rules, the universe itself, which is the outcome of the rules, is extremely complex.

"As above, so below" may be our hope for knowing what is unknowable to science and what often seems unknowable to our limited sensory apparatus. If the higher reality of Cosmo and the enlightened Self can be known, the knowledge might come from knowing the Self, where Cosmo (my term for God or truth) resides.

The essence of humankind is the essence of the universe. Whatever the universe is, we are; whatever the universe does, we do. If I believed in an anthropomorphic God, which I don't, I would add that whatever God wants, we want. The more one can recognize and experience the interconnections between separate layers of organization and separate entities, the more fulfilled and enlightened one will become. A meaningful and happy life comes from appreciating and harmonizing with the ongoing creative order of the Great Cosmo.

A more unified picture of the cosmos has emerged with each major advance in physics. In the seventeenth century Isaac Newton discovered the laws that unified celestial and terrestrial mechanics and gravitation, James Clark Maxwell's theories unified electrical and magnetic phenomena in the nineteenth century, and in the twentieth century, Einstein unified space and time as well as mass and energy. Recently, quantum science has further unified universal forces by showing that matter and the forces by which matter interacts are two aspects of the same underlying entity.

Perhaps the quest for enlightenment is simply an awareness of the universe evolving toward a recapturing of the unity lost before the Big Bang. Underlying the goal to improve our position is the desire to have infinite power and knowledge by unifying with the superior being who has it all. There is no satisfaction until that being is us, but understand that that being is already manifested in each of us, and what we want we already have.

CHAPTER 2

IDENTIFICTIONS—WHO AM I?

The Quest Begins with Separation

There is much talk today about the importance of unity and oneness. Unity may be humankind's goal and destiny, but the connections that lead to unity can't be formed without separation; without separation there is nothing to unify.

The uniting of Self and other requires first knowing and accepting the separate self. Although on a cosmic level interconnections operate to a profound degree, at the gross level of organic life, mortal humans cannot escape the fact that we are separate beings. I am not you, I am not the sky, and no matter how I might try to merge with whatever, I can only be the separate being that I am. A thought cannot occur without being isolated from other thoughts and experiences.

The viability of every plant or animal cell depends not only on maintaining a protective cell wall or cell membrane, but also on maintaining its interactions with the greater organism. Even the many organelles within the cell, such as the power-generating mitochondria, are enclosed in permeable membranes that allow for an exchange of nutrients. The unity of the whole depends on the diversity of its parts. The different role each part plays is essential to the whole—a muscle cell, a nerve cell, and each hemisphere of the brain serve different purposes even while cooperating for the benefit of the greater whole. Individual schoolteachers, each isolated in their own classroom, play a unique role, but collaboration will better allow all teachers to meet their common goal of preparing students for life.

Separation results whenever one course of action is chosen and another is rejected, or when value judgments determine one thing as right and another as wrong. Separation is a fact of life. I am as much about separateness as I am about unity. The state of separation means that judgments and the recognition of limits and boundaries are also very much a part of our lives, which brings a whole host of other problems which will be addressed throughout this book.

Distinctions must obviously be made between what is good and what is not. Whenever a judgment is made, a boundary is formed between the authentic Self and the other which I define as anything outside the Self, and this boundary becomes a barrier to what I call unity consciousness. This is the consciousness of connections between Self and other, a conscious state void of separation, of being-in-time rather than dwelling in the past or future. It seems that people spend their entire lives trying to find their way in a forest of separate experiences filled with the never-ending task of understanding how the trees comprise the forest. This Polarity Paradox of separation and unity, the one and the many, of Self and other, has vexed philosophers for centuries. How can unity consciousness be attained if oneness includes separation?

The never-ending challenge is to find the balance between separation and unity. The dog goes round and round chasing its tail and never being able to catch it, for not only can subject never catch object, it is also the subject we are after. But the chase is never-ending because to recognize that I am, I have to recognize that I am not, to recognize what I am, I have to recognize what I am not.

Trapped in a confused state of paradoxes and contradictions, a dualistic mode of thinking sees the world in simplistic terms of good and evil, right or wrong, black or white, ignoring the many nuances in between. This kind of thinking traps us in a secure prison of prejudices and generalizations that fails to recognize that, for instance, because I am at times reasonable and at other times unreasonable certainly doesn't mean that I am a permanently unreasonable person.

The mind-body separation is another form of dualism that is a source of conflict. No one knows who is in charge; mind wants to break free, whereas matter resists expansion and freedom. The failure to resolve the conflict between mind and body causes the perception of both disunity and insignificance to be responsible for the development of a monstrous ego swelled with false notions of self-importance. Failing to understand interdependence of body and mind leads to the distortion of natural tendencies, which then find unnatural expressions dangerous to Self and other.

In our first seconds of existence, we experience what will become a lifelong struggle to enjoy the freedom of independence while yearning for security. A newborn baby wails in protest as it leaves the familiar serenity and comfort of its mother's womb. It is tough to release the security of oneness found in your place of origin, the place you own. The world now becomes a lonely place. But being born is the first step toward participation in the process of evolving toward self-realization in the grand reconciliation of extremes.

For the remainder of our lives, we will try to regain the sense of unity we felt when we were one with the world of the womb. But with maturity, we also learn to appreciate separation, which is central to existence. Entry into the strange new world of separation offers infinite possibilities to experience the unique and wonderful world of sensory experience. Without separation there of course would be nothing to sense. Separation from certain elements is vital for continued existence. Muggers, swindlers, and wild beasts can do a number on you, and remaining separate from them is not only acceptable, it is highly encouraged.

Selfish concerns and awareness of separation, rather than unity, often seem to dominate the affairs of everyday life. Nations are torn apart by civil wars, Islam is divided between Shiites and Sunnis, Christianity is split between Catholics and Protestants, and the partisan divide between political parties seems insurmountable. The experience of separation misinterpreted becomes the Myth of the Super Me.   The myth that one can stand alone on the mountaintop only hastens the crash to the bottom.

Dualistic thinking is especially apparent in the Abrahamic religions that separate the material from the spiritual and the human from nature, and believe that God and Truth are external to the natural world. The idea that bodily functions and desires are somehow involved in spiritual warfare with a divine soul has resulted in discrimination and neurosis, and has contributed to the belief that mental disorders are without physical causes but are often simply due to making the wrong choices. Fortunately, science now recognizes the interrelationship of chemical, environmental, and genetic components that contribute to sexual orientation, to happiness and depression, alcoholism, and many other mental and physical conditions.

"Identifictions" and Other Myths

Everything that is "wrong" with us, every hang-up, neurosis, and attachment, every barrier to psychological and often physical well-being stems from the perception that we stand alone, incomplete and disconnected not only from the greater whole but from each other.

The perception of separation, and the reliance on the outside world for survival give rise to a false belief in a personal identity that is distorted and limited by its attachment to Positions and Possessions. People mistakenly believe that self-identity—indeed, their entire life's purpose—depends on social and professional status, political and religious positions, and place of residence. I refer to these, along with belief systems, values, memories, and dreams, as Positions. Throughout the book, I refer to material wealth, race and physical appearance as Possessions.

This false identification of self—this *fiction* that the essence of who I am, my personal value, meaning and purpose, depends on Positions and Possessions, I refer to as the Myth of Identifiction.

The perception of being separate and incomplete, and the dependence on the material world gives rise to the Myth of the Perfect Place which holds that truth and value are found in things and places external to the Self and that only matter matters. A major source of nagging stress is the belief that somewhere outside the Self there is a perfect missing piece that includes the perfect Positions and Possessions that will satisfy all desires, and provide happiness and the truth of who we are.

These two related myths depend on yet another myth; the Myth of the Missing Piece which is the illusion that to be fulfilled, to realize full potential, I must find the right role to play, according to the right script, have the right stuff at the right time in the right place, and the sooner the better. This is the false belief that personal value, purpose and identity depend on finding missing pieces that are external to individual consciousness.

Our unavoidable hang-up is the notion that who we are—the subjective Self—depends on what we have, where we are, and what we have done; in other words, the *objective self*. The belief that only matter matters convinces us that personal identity depends on a definable, measurable, objectified reality which then confuses us into thinking that the authentic Self is an objective entity to be defined, measured and compared.

The empirical ego that springs from the struggle to survive in the physical world sees matter as the highest form of existence. Physical matter plays such an obviously dominant role in our lives that we easily succumb to the delusion that truth of God and Self is found out there somewhere among all the other physical objects, albeit in some place and time other than the here and now. Personal identity is seen as an impersonal object dependent on things rather than as a subjective conscious awareness with the power of choice. The ego-self identifies with possessions and the physical realms, since we look at our bodies and think these corporeal vessels are the sum of who we are.

As separate material creatures trapped in space-time, with reality limited to those things that can be defined by outwardly directed senses, we become convinced that only physical existence is real. Since the conscious mind and nervous system can only sense the material world, things we can sense naturally take precedence over things we cannot. With a sensory system that depends on external stimuli, and that are incapable of sensing the inner authentic Self, we naturally emphasize external, tangible reality.

External stimuli obviously provide the wonderful pleasures we enjoy. Sensory stimulation is where it's at. Happiness is enjoying a juicy steak, lounging in a hot tub, and experiencing fantastic sex. The more the senses are stimulated, the more real life appears. If it can't be sensed, then it doesn't exist, as far as humans are concerned.

Anything that can't directly affect the senses is immaterial, irrelevant, and of no matter, matter being defined as anything that has weight and takes up space. To humans, *only matter matters*, therefore, we wrongly believe that for something to have any worth, for even the Self to matter, it must be material. If something is of great importance we say it matters a lot. We have the expression backward, as we do so many things. Since visible matter is only five percent of the universe,[1] if something is important, we should really say it doesn't matter.

Religions hold to the belief that God is all mighty in importance, and God's essence certainly isn't material. Nevertheless, the concept of a nonmaterial God is difficult to accept, since one might conclude that God, being immaterial and therefore of no matter, and incapable of being sensed, is nonsense. It's no thing should really mean it's important. The human's entire existence seems to revolve around making a big deal out of nothing—or near nothing. Instead of telling my wonderful wife, "You mean everything to me and you matter so much," To show her my love I should really tell her, "You mean nothing to me, you don't mat-

---

[1] Lee Smolin, The Trouble with Physics, p. 16

ter at all."

Since just about everything that supports life comes from material things, it is entirely natural that the false belief arises that the only way to find happiness and a meaningful life is to find and acquire the right things, take physical action, and look outside the Self for answers, including the answer to who we think we are as a person. Yes, time, space, material, and separation are important to life, but over-emphasizing them hinders connections with all forms of the other. The idea that even personal identity depends on acquiring Positions and Possessions leads to a disconnect from the feeling of being present. Unless primary importance is first placed on the Self of the present, it is difficult to love the other. However, everyone knows the aphorism, "The answer lies within." I would add that the answer is found by knowing that the within is in the without, Self is found in other.

All of the myths I've described result in an inauthentic sense of personal identity as well as a more shallow life experience.

The Danger of Positions and Possessions

Positions and Possessions become symbols, roles and props in the play of life. The roles we assume—teacher, parent, spouse, expert—and the props we use—money, cars, belief systems, associations—and the corresponding social status these things give us, all contribute to personal identity but as we will see, our authentic Self lies beyond Positions and Possessions. Our symbolic lives not only build walls of separation between Self and other but serve as barriers to recognizing the perfection of the authentic Self.

The inauthentic, ego-self is defined and measured for convenient placement in a box, and is then arranged on a shelf with other possessions. All the time and effort wasted beautifying and adorning the body, and the ego, reminds me of someone who is more impressed with the box containing the gift and with the wrapping on the package than with what is inside. We pay so much attention to the box that the box is mistaken for the Self. In some cases, the wrapping may actually bring more pleasure than the contents, and this may be the reason some of us spend so much time wrapping our identities with images and symbols, completely ignoring the gift of consciousness. The fancy packaging and fancy words may hide an empty container.

The problem arises that since the Self is immaterial and can't be measured, we are confused not only as to its value, but as to its very existence. Our inadequate solution to this frustrating problem of not being able to define our identity, our Self, is to base its value on things that can be measured. These tangible things become symbols for who we are and become a phony measure of self-worth. I can count the dollars I have in the bank, the cars parked in the garage, and the diplomas on the wall but I can't measure the immaterial self that I am or the relationships I form with the other.

Positions and Possessions become mere images and symbols; houses, cars, and clothes assume more importance as status symbols than as functional items. The purpose of the body is to wrap and trap experience like a glass traps water and a balloon traps air. The type of container, along with its size and shape, are irrelevant—as long as it doesn't leak. Don't throw out the wine because of a spot on the glass. It is the mind within the container that harbors, organizes, and does the experiencing.

People identify so much with Positions and Possessions that when any of these things are criticized, lost or damaged it is taken as a personal assault. A scratch on the car is a scratch on the Self. Identifictions lead to the feeling that if Positions or Possessions are lost, then personal identity is also lost. Most of us have had that profoundly empty feeling after losing some prized possession—a loved one, a cell phone, a cherished belief which I include as a possession, or perhaps having been separated from a companion in a foreign city. Losing such things gives one the horrible feeling that a piece of the Self has been lost. It seems that a little bit of identity has been chipped away with each loss of attachment, along with the loss of security, control, power and perhaps even life's meaning and purpose.

Symbols Confine Truth

Symbols limit God and the Self.

The unity we crave, and the identity we look for, is limited by the unavoidable measuring and comparing of one thing with another. Profound connections with the other, and with the wonder of being, can only be experienced by moving beyond the rigid definitions and symbols of language and conceptualization, and beyond the confines of conventional boundaries. Conceptualizing limits the infinite nature of experience with defined boundaries and measured differences. As soon as a moment is measured or defined, the moment and everything it contains is limited, including the Self.

The use of language is perhaps the most prevalent method of confining reality in a way the human mind can comprehend. A thing has no meaning until it is defined by words, this is the significance of the Genesis metaphor in which Adam gives names to the creatures in the Garden. But by judging which words to use we are forced to evaluate and measure the worth of one thing as compared with another, and symbols then become boundaries that separate us from experience, that separate Self from other.

Words can only describe a world of duality that is broken into separate bits of this and that. Unfortunately, humans operate under the illusion that this world of separate identities is the only reality. We live in a world of words that causes us to ignore the larger, unified picture, the undefinable reality beneath the symbol. Symbols, especially words, help us to manage reality by ordering and categorizing our world, but in so doing we freeze and limit experience, preventing us from flowing and integrating with the process of being. Defining is confining.

If there is any area of life, or any institution, that should penetrate the symbols that disguise reality, it is religion. Religion offers the hope of forming a profound connection with the other in the pursuit of unifying subject and object. Unfortunately, religions employ symbols, metaphors, and rituals to describe the indescribable unity with the truth they seek. Spiritual teachings, often lost in rituals and dogma, lead to a shallow, inauthentic experience of a separate rather than a unified reality that Jean-Paul Sartre would describe as a bad-faith identity with things.

All the major religions pretend to believe in the reality of one God, but religious practitioners commit the sacrilege of idol worship. Regardless of our religious or political beliefs, we are all guilty of the sacrilege of idol worship by becoming so attached to Positions and Positions, beliefs, routines, and rituals, and words that, in addition to becoming part of our very identity, become false gods that break the cosmic connection.

I recently read a sad account of a young girl who was denied the sacrament in a Catholic church because an allergy didn't allow her to eat the wheat wafers that represented the body of Christ. What a tragedy when symbols and rituals become the reality, but this is our everyday life, where the Infinite has been trapped in a body of symbols. Think of the huge controversy between early Christians and Jews that surrounded the rite of circumcision. God declared in Genesis 17:11 that circumcision was a sign of a covenant between man and God, so of course all true believers had to be snipped. This absurd symbol of faith consumed a ridiculous amount of time and energy and became a major topic in Paul's New Testament letters as he tried to deemphasize the importance of this symbol, which had become more important than the symbol's underlying reality which is to lose Identifictions and false attachments. Give me a break. Does a loving God care whether my penis is clipped or not?

An example of the importance of symbols was driven home to me a few years ago when I visited York Minster, England's finest Gothic cathedral. While marveling at the vastness of this cathedral and its fabulous carvings and magnificent stained glass windows, I was struck by the silent reverence of the crowds, almost as if God itself was hiding somewhere in the nave. Struck by natural urges brought on by morning coffee, I headed for the restroom where I found people noisily chatting away in their normal, very secular way. I couldn't help but think how we tend to compartmentalize religion and spiritual feelings, evidently deciding that God's compartment is not in the toilet.

Now, don't get me wrong. Symbols, rituals, and traditions

definitely serve a purpose by creating an atmosphere that encourages spirituality. A spiritual mood may be enhanced by meditating, praying, or sharing within a group, or listening to music and being surrounded by religious icons. Participating in a Japanese Zen tea ceremony, where every movement and gesture are symbolic of the principles of Buddhism, helps to foster a spiritual mood. The Japanese tea ceremony, like all aspects of life, can be experienced on different levels: aesthetic, sensory, and spiritual. A good life is enhanced by integrating levels and being able to distinguish between symbol and reality such as seeing a car for what it is, a means of transportation rather than as a part of personal identity. To a greater or lesser degree, happiness and spiritual experiences are thought to depend on Positions and Possessions, and we are afraid that if we lose these things, we will also lose happiness.

Jesus's concern was to align his life and thought with universal truth. He didn't think of himself as a man limited by the Identifictions of Positions or Possessions, but rather, if he was enlightened, he saw himself as a manifestation of the universal creative force, as we all are, regardless of our religion. How unfortunate that so often the image, symbol, and object of Jesus the man is worshiped, rather than the truth he represents, which, though universal, is manifested in infinite ways. Worshiping of symbols is considered idolatry by followers of the Abrahamic religions.

When asked which commandment was the most important, Jesus responded, "Love the Lord your God with all your heart and with all your soul and with all your mind. And the second is like it. You shall love your neighbor as yourself." Jesus, like all people of The Way,[2] was all about inclusion rather than exclusion. The cosmos includes Self and Neighbor, separate but equally worthy of love. This message of unity is also central to the teachings of the Eastern religions of Hinduism, Buddhism, and Taoism.

---

[2]   the path to higher consciousness

We get stuck in the shallows by relying on symbols and concepts to define and split reality into pieces, but intuitively we know that we are intimately connected with an undefined greater reality. Jesus showed how he didn't confuse reality with the symbol when he broke with Jewish heritage and convention by healing on the Sabbath. By speaking in parables, Jesus demonstrated his understanding that Truth is limited by the use of symbols.

Just as personal identity and the authentic Self is limited by definitions, so God (truth, reality) is limited in the same way. For anything to exist, it must stand by itself as a separate entity so it would seem to follow that if God exists, it must be a separate entity since "Exist," from the Latin *exitere*, originally meant "to stand out." Even though God is incomprehensible, we still attempt the impossible by boxing it in with definitions and descriptions so as to give God attributes that make sense, and sensible *things* have to be separated, and therefore, limited. But to separate God is to separate reality. The concept of God becomes a victim of thinking in materialistically measured terms. In the words of the great Protestant theologian Paul Tillich, "It is as atheistic to affirm the existence of God as to deny it. God is being itself, not a being." In other words, God is not an entity but rather is the ground-of-being itself.

"Thou shalt have no graven images before me." The Second Commandment suggests that it is sacrilege to believe that God is some external thing that can be conceptualized, controlled, and chipped away to be confined to a certain place and time. Experience is limited, as is the nature of the authentic Self and Cosmo by futile attempts to measure, locate, define, and compare. A god that can be conceptualized and located has lost omnipotence and omnipresence, and the truth held by a "savior" or "prophet" is limited when the person, such as Jesus or Mohammed is worshipped, rather than the truth represented.

The Second Commandment goes way beyond just forbidding the worship of statues and images. It asks us not to confuse the symbol with the reality. I believe the purpose of the Second Commandment is to elevate the subjective I AM experience of the perfect present rather than to hold the false belief that happiness, meaning and personal identity are found by worshiping the symbols of Positions and Possessions. We are putting faith in that new, high-tech camera, flashy car, high-paying position or religion or political position to fill the void left by the failure to see our relationship to the perfect order of the Great Cosmo. The car is not the Self.

Since God can't be seen, the church is filled with symbols to worship, such as crosses and statues, that represent God. And as if this wasn't enough, this infinite being is restricted to the pages of a book called the Torah, Bible, or Koran. Finally, His Infinite Nothingness has been captured and is now closer to being a something that can actually be defined and captured, though also being limited in the process. Since we can't see our Self, we fill our garage and house with possessions, and decorate our walls with documents and photographs that we think of as our identity. A false image of God is created in the same way we create a false image of Self.

The Myth of the Perfect Place not only has given a mythic God a position separate and outside of us, but a position way high up in the heavens where it can look down on lowly humans. Height occupies so much symbolic importance that we have common idioms such as, "being on top of things," "things are looking up," "stand tall," "pinnacle of success." Humans, in the attempt to be god-like and on top of things, feel superior when they occupy "superior" positions from which they can look down on the "lower" classes. A 2005 survey of the height of Fortune 500 CEOs showed that 30 percent were at least 6'2", whereas only 4 percent of the general public reaches that height[3] and from 1900 to 2016, the tallest United States presidential candidate has won 20 out of 28 times. Gigantic, towering cathedrals and churches, some larger in area than a football field, were constructed at fantastic costs with the idea in mind that a bigger and taller edifice reflects a stronger commitment to God.

---

[3]   Gladwell, Malcolm, 2005, "Blink"

Areas that reach deeply into our lives, such as religion and politics, are especially sensitive subjects, and the more absolute and dogmatic the position, the stronger the Identifiction and the rejection of the other's position. It is because of the false reliance on Positions for a sense of self that such topics have become too sensitive and threatening for polite conversation.

Symbols can't be avoided and do serve as an organizing and filtering bridge between reality and the individual. But sometimes we get so hung up on the symbol, whether in the form of Positions, Possessions, rituals, conventions, belief systems or just words, that the symbol is mistaken for the reality and the experience is lost. The flow of a discussion often gets bogged down, and the underlying message is lost, over petty, long-winded debates over definitions. Since the human is defined as a symbolizing, conceptualizing animal of the highest order, the best we can do is to minimize the negative impact of living symbolically by, at times, recognizing the underlying reality.

The inauthentic and shallow experience of over valuing symbols is, in part, the consequence of depending on external authority for truth, and accepting the dominant reality of separateness and the myth that to have anything of value, including God's approval, one must search outside the Self. This separation can lead to feelings of unworthiness and alienation from Self and other, for other can't be loved without loving the Self. It is perfectly okay to want material objects, but don't confuse the symbol with the reality.

In the attempt to overcome the insecurity and fear of separation lies the temptation to seek refuge in the blind attachment to the authority of religions, or a politician's polemical promises of Utopia. For security, boundaries of all kinds are constructed, physical, psychological and cultural. Breaking boundaries and shaking off the shackles of tradition and ritual can be a lonely journey in the search for truth.

Can't Get No Satisfaction

> Modern man, if he dared to be articulate about his concept of heaven, would describe a vision which would look like the biggest department store in the world, showing new things and gadgets, and himself having plenty of money with which to buy them. He would wander around open-mouthed in this heaven of gadgets and commodities, provided only that there were ever more and newer things to buy, and perhaps that his neighbors were just a little less privileged than he.
>
> —Erich Fromm, *Man in Capitalistic Society*

In the song that made them famous, the Rolling Stones cry out, "I can't get no satisfaction." Even though things are pretty darned good, we are always hoping that with the acquisition of more possessions and superior positions that things will get even better. The instant one desire is met, another one takes its place. In fact, all the new things that continually emerge from civilizations create needs and desires we didn't even know we had.

It is human nature to hope that we will discover that perfect answer, the perfect solution that will lead to the Super Connection with the Absolute. In fact it is hope that many life-satisfaction studies show as having the highest relationship to happiness.[4]

Here's the problem: if we think that well-being is determined by the expectation that situations will improve, then of course it is more difficult to feel grateful for one's present position. For the most part, the future goodies we crave no more hold the answer than do the goodies we presently have. As a kid who had just learned to type, the joy I felt as I hammered away on the

---

[4] Park, Peterson, and Seligman; 2004. "Strengths of character and well-being." *Journal of Social and Clinical Psychology*, 23, 603–619.

family's clunky old Remington typewriter, was probably equal to that of today's youth who receives the flashiest new computer. It used to be that all we expected from our twenty-one-inch black and white television set was news, old movies, quiz shows, and sitcoms. Now that we have a sixty-inch set we expect to have Wi-Fi, Bluetooth, 3-D, HD, a DVR capable of recording four programs simultaneously, and a satellite dish that pulls in hundreds of stations. A bad movie is still a bad movie regardless of the size of the TV. The problem arises when expectations interfere with the appreciation of the present. Attachment to the idea that dreams of happiness and meaning are things found just around the corner turns the wonder of life into a never-ending search for symbols that never match reality. Today is always here, as I Am, tomorrow never comes.

While striving for more and better things seems to be part of human nature, we often hope and strive for the wrong things, and that's just it, "thingness" is the problem. Things are so much on our minds we don't even know a word other than "things" to use for what we want.

The false belief that only matter matters, and the myth that identity is based on Positions and Possessions, give rise to the belief that more matter is better. Since the primary need for connection with Self and other can't be met by pursuing any thing material such as Positions and Possessions, we engage in the foolish chase to acquire more of everything thinking that the void left by the break with the I Am of the perfect present can be filled if only we can acquire enough stuff.

It is pretty obvious why size and quantity matter. The mistaken belief that my identity and my very survival depend on things leads me to believe that the more things I have and the bigger they are, the stronger my identity and the better will be the quality of my life. A well-stocked freezer, a large house, a sizable bank account, and years of seniority with the firm all provide a sense of security. No matter what it is, the smaller it gets, the closer it is to being nonexistent.

Associating God with enormity, infinity, eternity, and absolute power may contribute to the subconscious feeling that in some way we will be closer to satisfying the fundamental desire to unite with the eternal if we have bigger houses, bigger bodies, bigger breasts, bigger sexual organs, and ever more powerful cars. Americans have mega churches, mega houses, monster trucks, gigantic big-screen televisions, and skyscrapers as tall as mountains. We are convinced that to be really happy we have to be the big puddle rather than the tiny drop. The word "enormous" has over 200 synonyms.

But more stuff creates more problems, with gain comes loss. The rich and famous lose their privacy and freedom, the brilliant scholar becomes conceited, arrogant and opinionated. Now that I am so rich and famous, and have so many things, I need a bigger house and I have to build bigger and better and more elaborate defensive walls and meaner dogs to protect it all. I must construct elaborate psychological walls to protect my fragile ego from the attacks of those who covet, criticize or demean me and my possessions.

The problem is that the universe consists of an infinite variety of things that lead to unending confusion as to which things to choose. And no matter how many shelves I put up, the spaces always seem filled to overflowing. We spend the first half of our lives accumulating things and the second half trying to get rid of them.

Americans have more stuff than any society in history, so much they can't find room in their oversized houses to store it. The $24 billion self-storage industry has nearly 49,000 storage facilities, more than all the rest of the world combined. The big question is whether people are happier and have more meaningful lives because of their mountains of consumer goods.

Even though people in many countries are relatively better off now than they have been in the past—at least regarding their health and material life—time and again studies have shown that personal happiness is no greater now that it was in the 1950s. Yes, we have a lot of fun toys and labor-saving devices, but the more we have, the more we want and the more we expect. In his book *The High Price of Materialism*, Tim Kasser, professor of psychology at Knox College in Illinois, provides empirical evidence that a life based on materialistic values increases the risk of depression, anxiety, and ill health. So I may have financial success and admiring sycophants, but I may lack authenticity or genuine happiness. Authentic individuals will see fancy titles, trophies, and material wealth for what they are: empty shells that disguise a sad, disconnected and shadow self.

The false belief that we're dissatisfied because we don't have enough of the right stuff, leads to the desire to acquire and to the pointless pursuit of perfection. These desires are so pervasive and often subtle that we are oblivious to their subtle interference with our state of mind. I am writing this after having taken a morning walk in the northern California town of Willits. During the walk I commented to my wife on the attractiveness of a little garden set in a grove of giant redwoods. The first thought on seeing the pretty little purple flowers took me right out of the present as I thought how nice those flowers would look blooming in my garden. In a way, this was good because I began to think that when I got home I would begin weeding a long-neglected section of the garden, where I would plant some of those same beautiful little purple flowers for a border. This gave me a very affordable and easily attainable goal, something to look forward to, and an easy way to add a little meaning to my activities for the day. So dissatisfaction with one's present condition can be a good thing.

But the desire to acquire won't give up. The next day, as I was dropping my son off, I admired the driveway and sidewalk next to his house. I wished that my driveway had the same look, since I have long thought of having it redone. Next to the driveway I admired an orange tree laden with fruit and wished that my orange tree would produce like that. You see, we can hardly look at anything without asking, do I want this? How can I afford it? How can I get it? How does it compare with what I have? And if I am not possessed by the desire to possess, I may still engage in the game of evaluating as I reject certain yards as being unattractive. Each one of these little comparisons and evaluations eats away, ever so slightly, at the enjoyment of the present process of being. There was good reason for Jesus to tell his disciples, "You lack one thing: go sell all that you have and give it to the poor, and you will have treasure in heaven; and come, follow me." Mark 10:21.

A disturbing feature of modern society is that as things get bigger, faster and easier, the contrast required as a condition of existence becomes harder to find. Play all the time and play becomes work. A person who takes drugs to get high, finding that highs become lows, takes ever-increasing amounts to get high or turns to stronger drugs. What eventually happens is that ever-increasing size and quantity no longer increases value. Soon there is no more space to store the goodies, the expansive yard just takes too much time and money to keep up. The new dream home is a small beach cottage or even a condo. The huge and powerful muscle cars of the 1960s gave way to the economical compact cars of the '70s. The bigger things become, the more powerful the urge to get small—but only for a while, and soon the desire returns for big and powerful.

If bigger, faster and more doesn't satisfy, then the quest for the best is on for some brand name that offers more status and higher quality. The new luxury Lexus, soon taken for granted as just another means of transportation, has to be replaced by a Ferrari. Research has shown that when self-esteem is low, when people feel powerless, they are more likely to buy expensive brand-name objects. When I was a struggling college student, my transportation was a very unimpressive and rather slow six-horsepower Lambretta motor scooter. I'm sure I got as much enjoyment out of leaning into the curves on the winding road leading into the redwoods in Big Basin State Park on my gutless Lambretta as the guy who roared past me on a powerful Harley-Davidson. But I don't think it's really power, riches or fame that we're after in the quest for more, faster, bigger and better positions and possessions. So what is it we want?

Positions and Possessions certainly cannot be ignored; matter matters, can't survive without it. Without material there is nothing to experience. However, authentic identity, along with happiness, fades away when tied to the transience of material, to Positions and Possessions. Things can never satisfy the higher need for meaning and authenticity. Not knowing how to satisfy the greater need for unity, we think the answer is that we need bigger things, or more things, or we just haven't found the right things.

I'm afraid that our technologically driven digital society is headed toward even greater attachment to things until we won't be able to distinguish between the self and the objects we create. I'm reminded of what the monster told Dr. Frankenstein, "You are my creator but I am your master."

Well, I we've come to the end of the chapter and I still haven't answered the question, "Who am I?" We'll get there but to know who I am I do have to know what I am not.

Chapter 3

The Empire of the Super Me

The Empire of the Super Me

We all want to be number one, to be the Super Me in control and on top of things. A primary human need is to feel uniquely important, valued, needed and appreciated. Oneness is what I want but often I can't see beyond my own nose so, rather than being one with you, it is easier and more obvious to think the answer is for me to be number one all by myself.

We would like the engraving on our tombstone to read, "Here lies Me, the world's absolute best, the most important, most unforgettable and popular person ever." According to Friedrich Nietzsche, these desires are expressions of humankind's Will to Power.

To satisfy these needs, we seek some way to not only stand out from others, but to stand above them, although sometimes, uniqueness itself is seen as superiority. No one wants to be just another cog in a machine; being only equal or average doesn't cut it. We want to excel in some area: an athlete wants to win, not just play the game; kids on little league teams dream of playing professional ball; a reporter dreams of winning a Pulitzer. But at the same time, humans are faced with the familiar conundrum of wanting to stand out while also wanting to fit in.

Humans mistakenly think, perhaps subconsciously, that the answer to their problems lies in uniting with or actually becoming that one almighty singular thing or God that will finally relieve the anxiety of choice and satisfy all desires. If we can't become all-powerful and all-knowing, and if we can't acquire enough things then we can, at least in our fantasies and mind perhaps share in the glory of association with the Absolute, whether the glory is in the form of a supernatural being, particular ideology or in the belief in the Super Me.

But even being number one isn't enough. We want to be the all-time absolute winner. As I said before, we're never satisfied, always wanting more. The world's number one tennis player isn't satisfied with just winning Wimbledon; she wants to win the Grand Slam. Even then, she still isn't satisfied until she wins more tournaments than any other player in history. Just give me more, more fame, more money, more fun, more knowledge, more contentment, more possessions, more friends, more sex, and especially, more time. And the bigger my things, the faster my things, the more things I have, the better I am and the closer I am to being the absolute best.

Even when we are on the same side, everyone thinking just like me—members of the same church or political party, or on the same team, we want our position in the group to be just a little higher, a little more important. I may claim to want equality, but I have to honestly admit to defining sometimes minute differences between us, and to making countless little judgments that in some way place me above you. I still think that in ways that really count, I am just a little bit better than others that the shelf where I keep my identity is the top shelf. I must feel that my value is superior to yours. Steve Jobs may have been smarter than me but in the overall picture I am just as good as Jobs because I get along better with people. Oh, sure, I know that we are all created equal and all that, but deep down, I am reluctant to accept the value of your existence as really being equal to mine.

Some individuals elevate their position as a Super Me by actually placing themselves below others by saying something like, "My unique problems and minority status give me insights and perspectives that you can never understand, and which entitle me to special consideration." Perceived or real, these differences can become a badge of pride that offer a distinct identity while at the same time offering the security of belonging to a group that shares a similar unique status. These "misfits" see themselves as special individuals whose perceptive insights into the human condition gained from a condition of misery and misfortune place them apart from and above the crowd. The victim is absolved from the pressure of competing and the risk of failure since their perceived inferior/superior position depends on being on the bottom.

I do want to make it clear that there are many instances of handicaps and unusual circumstances that certainly justify special accommodations. I would also emphasize that, to one degree or another, at times, we all play the victim.

Even if we do capture what we think is the prize, we still feel incomplete and dissatisfied. Soon it is noticed how green the grass is on the other side of the fence and the chase for Utopia is resumed. When we do find the greener grass, we may discover it is filled with weeds, ticks, and poison oak.

We are often asked how we like something, and a typical response is, "Yeah, it's a good car, but the mileage could be better"; "My new camera takes great pictures, but it's too heavy"; "I love my husband, but he can be so critical;" Yeah, the Niagara Falls are spectacular, but you should see the Iguassu Falls." Put all of our reservations together, and what we are really saying is, "Yeah, life is pretty good, but it could be better; I could be happier; God has a few defects." This is the Myth of the Missing Piece. As the Greek poet Homer so wisely said, "The fool finds fault with a place. The fault is not there but in the mind."

I don't care what it is—the newest high-tech camera, the house of our dreams, or our present friend or lover—we will soon find something wrong with it. And that little defect or imperfection is what holds us back from making the Super Connection. The eternal challenge is to appreciate the moment while working to build a better mousetrap.

Humans seem to revel in putting down individuals and

groups, and detailing what's wrong with the world. The list of things people are criticized and judged for includes preferences in music, art, literature, politics, you name it, the list is endless. Habitual criticism separates Self from other.

By putting others down, we are putting the Self down, because Self is other. Criticizing others, or boasting and believing in the Super Me, is over-compensation for a low self-image and feelings of inferiority. When others are seen as being stupid and inconsiderate, it is because we lack faith in our own intelligence and goodness and fail to accept our own shadow nature. Everything I dislike or criticize about you is really what I dislike about me, but I need a scapegoat—I need a hook for my hang-ups.

Individuals hoping to make the Super Connection, waiting for a permanent, perfect solution to their discontent may be reluctant to meaningfully commit to any connection. They are constantly remodeling their home or changing residences, changing spouses, buying new things. Never satisfied, they hesitate to make any commitment for fear of missing out on the best that is always yet to come, always around the next corner. Holding the worldview that somewhere there is a perfect mate may lead to problems in establishing meaningful relationships and to a life of loneliness and pessimism because unrealistic expectations in one area is likely to infect every area of their lives. To one degree or another, at one time or another, we all have this reluctance or fear to commit.

Tired of transitory pleasures and futile quests for happiness and meaning, we want to know where to find permanence. Our fundamental desire is to know and experience the Absolute. Our intuition that there is more than what we now have causes us to doubt the perfection of the moment, even though, as shall soon see, the object of our desire is to be satisfied with the moment.

My mother-in-law is lucky. She gets a hair permanent every few weeks. She looks forward to this. Even though the process should really be called a hair temporary, when you're one-hundred years old, you like the idea of getting *anything* that's permanent. I'm lucky because I have a *real* permanent—being bald, I'm happy for having at least something that is permanent.

Humans seem to inherently seek the security of permanence and immutability of some kind. This futile search is the Problem of the P's—the pointless pursuit of positions, possessions, places, permanence and perfection.

We want it all, we want all the pieces back together. The problem is that we don't know where or what the All is, mistakenly thinking that whatever it is, it must be a thing out there somewhere, always somewhere other than where we are.

We're All Big Shots

We may disguise elitism as simple preferences, but when we are conscious of a preference for one thing, we at least subconsciously reject another choice as being of lesser value. And what is preferred above all else is the self, which always puts the not-self in an inferior light. Self-worth is always elevated above worth of the other. The importance of a healthy sense of self-worth can not be underestimated but the arrogance of thinking that my universe is not only separate from yours, but also superior casts the Other as a threatening force that needs to be fenced out, eliminated, or converted.

The problem is that the realm of the inauthentic self forever expands as one goes through life collecting opinions, biases, judgments, and Positions and Possessions to place in the basket mislabeled as the Self. And the larger the inauthentic self becomes, the smaller and less recognizable is the authentic Self.

In truth, the more differences I see between Self and other, the *weaker* is my identity. The authentic Self recognizes *similarities*. The security, control, and power that come from putting ourselves at the top of the order is illusory.

The one way of the inauthentic Super Me destroys individuality, stops evolution, divides and conquers, and, carried to extremes, results in book-banning and burning, people-banning and burning, crusades, inquisitions, and bloody jihads.

The rise of the Super Me is of course over compensation for feelings of inadequacy and inferiority. To us humans, size and quantity matter. Identifying so much with material, and placing primary importance on externals, we can't help thinking of ourselves as tiny, insignificant pieces of matter that matter little in comparison to the greater entities like God, billionaires, celebrities, and the wise and scholarly experts with all their degrees and credentials.

We identify more with imperfection than perfection and then overcompensate by pretending to be the tough guys and the only smart ones on the planet. Nothing and no one meets our expectations. Feelings of inferiority arise primarily from a failure to meet the expectations of others, and from the many myths and Identifictions that we subscribe to that give us a false sense of authenticity.

So accustomed are we to feeling inferior that we take every opportunity to elevate ourselves by proudly announcing our accomplishments and victories while putting down everything and everyone around us. Criticism and rejection of the other is rejection of the Self, since Self and other are interdependent. The underlying reasons for excessive self-criticism and criticism of other is the same.

In the words of Spinoza, "All things follow from the necessity of the divine nature; so that whatsoever he deems to be hurtful and evil, and whatsoever, accordingly seems to him impious, horrible, unjust and base, assumes that appearance owing to his own disordered, fragmentary and confused view of the universe." Circumstances have been and always will be perfectly ordered according to nature's intent. Each particle of existence, each action, manifests and encompasses universal order and principle; every atom, every rock, every organism is linked in an infinite cosmic web, all perfectly ordered.

As a matter of survival, differences must be recognized and the individual must place primary value on personal Positions and Possessions. Corporations, nations, families, and individuals must look after their own interests. However, for civilization and the individual to advance, the way must be seen to resolving the Polarity Paradox by lowering the wall between Self and other.

Altruism died out with the divinely empathetic cave dweller who fed himself to the poor, starving saber-toothed tiger. There are real threats out there, threatening ideas in addition to physical dangers. You can never be certain whether those following footsteps belong to friend or foe. "Turn the other cheek" and "love your enemy" may be sound spiritual advice, but tell that to the mouse being chased by a cat or an elderly couple walking alone on a dark inner-city street. There is no room for compromise with a suicide bomber intent on blowing up a busload of innocent children.

Paradise is lost by dwelling on the glories of heaven while ignoring the valley below. But when you are on top—and we all think we are on top, even when we are on the bottom—how difficult it is to give credit to the supporting foundation. When Edmund Hillary conquered Mt. Everest, the last thing on his mind was the bottom of the mountain, but without the mountain base, he would not only have crashed down to earth, but there would have been no Everest to conquer. In fact, the historical record is filled with despots so attached to their lofty positions of power that they were inevitably brought down by the revolt of neglected citizens. Acceptance of the mountain bottom, acceptance of the dark side, nonbeing, and the Other leads to understanding, to love, and finally to unity consciousness. Corporate CEOs, presidents, and football quarterbacks have no purpose without a team, just as a creator has no existence without a creation and there can be no mountaintop without a mountain bottom.

Trouble arises and empires fall when one part sees itself as being more important than other parts, as when a star athlete on a basketball team hogs the ball, or nationalistic policies isolate a nation. In a relatively free market, a corporation will fail when it over-values profit to the neglect of the consumer. When the number one team loses respect for the ability of the other or dwells too much on holding the number one position, defeat is close at hand. Individual cells, organs and the individual are nothing without their interdependent relationship, and so it is with the branches of government, a corporation, and the members of a family. Communication, respect, and connections between each part and between the parts and the whole are essential.

The egotistically elevated view of our own personal value is analogous to one of our trillions of cells being convinced of its supreme importance. Suppose a few cells form a defensive coalition as protection from imaginary threats posed by other cells and organs they imagine are conspiring against them. Blood cells would knock on the doors of these paranoid cells. "Hey, I've got a delivery of oxygen and nutrients," they call out, to which the paranoid cells respond, "Sorry, I know you guys are out to get us, can't let you in." It is, of course, essential that cells form protective boundaries and cell membranes. Cells are like miniature cities, with their own power plants, food processing factories, control centers, and waste disposal systems, and all of these metabolic functions must be carried out satisfactorily in order to meet the needs of the organs and of the organism itself. For the cell to flourish it must link with other cells, just as the health of cities and nations depend on free trade between borders.

Humans, however, overemphasize their separate importance while ignoring their responsibility and connection to other levels of organization. It is so hard to look beyond the differences that have become our Identifictions, and so much easier to keep a safe distance from others by relating on a superficial level. The fight to maintain defensive walls to protect Self from other is found at all levels of existence: physical, biological, psychological, and societal. We are actually all on the same side yet pretending to be on opposite sides.

To be human is to emphasize separation, differences, and to see a world of limitations; to be divine is to see the common thread between Self and other, to be aware of the world of infinite possibilities and unlimited connections. The first step toward unity consciousness is to recognize Self in other by accepting that a common human nature transcends ethnic, gender, material or any other boundaries. Only hate and fear spring forth from ignorance of connections.

One might say that enlightened spirituality, or unity consciousness is the realization that nothing is actually something and something is nothing, which boils down to the discovery that I am not the big shot that I think I am, but then neither are you. The humility that I am nothing allows me to bring you into my world, and then together we become bigger shots than we ever thought possible. The most profound spiritual high is when you and I share the same wave length with the underlying understanding that your value is equal to mine. Jonathan Haidt, author of *The Righteous Mind*, concludes that happiness doesn't come from within but, rather, from between.

An overriding truth of existence seems to be that everything in the visible and invisible universe is inextricably interrelated — gravity, space-time, and not only are energy and matter related, as Einstein's equation $E = mc^2$ so simply states, they are equal. Inherent in humans is the faith, or intuitive belief, that by connecting with this greater unified reality, this unbroken continuum, a level of being will be experienced far beyond what we know.

Everything depends on its relationship to everything else — it is the mind of the human that separates one thing from the other. The Will to Unify is the desire for the super connection between Self and other that underlies the fundamental pursuit to transcend the barrier between the individual and a greater reality.

The aim of Eastern religions such as Buddhism, Taoism, and Hinduism is to experience interconnectedness by transcending the separate world of the Super Me's isolated ego. In the East, the vision of a separate world is called avidya, which means "ignorance," and is seen as the product of a disturbed mind. In the words of Asvaghosa, a first-century Buddhist scholar, "When the mind is disturbed, the multiplicity of things is produced, but when the mind is quieted, multiplicity disappears." And in the Bible, Colossians 3:14 reminds us that "love binds everything together in perfect harmony."

Unity Embraces Separation

Paradoxically, the very drive for unity and connections that can overcome intolerance, stereotyping and narcissism can also be their cause, resulting in even more divisiveness. Misguided attempts to destroy barriers and to open borders often leads to the creation of new barriers. An idea carried to extremes becomes its opposite, truth becomes falsehood, unity changes to separation—and humans have a great tendency to go to extremes.

Religious and political leaders are often advocates of unity and tolerance, but sadly, at times, do just the opposite by transforming unity into separation. We find in religion and politics the mythological claim to the perfect place, which leads to the conviction that there is only one true path to paradise and salvation. The unifying belief in one God, or in one political point of view, soon becomes the insistence that because my way is superior, everyone must follow me. The priest and politician both believe in God and the devil, heaven and hell. For the politician, the political opposition represents the devil, for the priest, the devil resides in foreign religions.

Once again, using the analogy of body cells, Liberals, the seekers of unity, would tear down the cellular membranes that provide structure to the body, collapsing it into an amorphous, one-celled blob. Conservatives, as defenders of individualism, would shore up the cell walls with steel girders, thus starving the body of nutrients. If unrestrained, the actions of both sides of the political spectrum, would work against their professed worthy goals of freedom and unity. The unintended consequence of each approach would eventually eliminate unique identity by making the two into one.

Heated political debates argue the issue of equality of opportunity versus equality of outcome, or simply equity vs. equality. Advocates for each position accuse the other of intolerance. A fundamental difference between Conservatives and Liberals centers on identifying the degree of economic, social, and educational inequality that should be tolerated in civilized society.

The difficulty in finding solutions rests with the inherent tendency toward the polarized thinking that rigid boundaries separate two mutually exclusive poles. When carried to an extreme, equality of outcome results in a system that fails to reward initiative and responsibility, whereas the opposite extreme promoting equality of opportunity may lead to exploitation of the poor by the rich and powerful. Carried too far, as is often the case, each approach increases separation and inequality at the expense of unity.

Just as the conflicting forces of expansion and contraction seem to put the universe at war with itself, so humans are engaged in an internal civil war of a similar nature between separation and unity. I construct psychological and physical walls for protection from outside threats at the same time I seek protection and companionship by uniting with other members of my tribe.

Just as the body's cells, organs and organ systems are inextricably linked with a greater level of organization called the human organism, so each individual is linked to greater organizational communities of the family, neighborhood, city, nation, world, and universe. Each level consists of separate pieces, and though separate—like the pixels in a digital picture—the separate parts can't be forced into one place. The many cells in the body can't somehow be squished into one giant cell any more than a digitized picture can consist of just one pixel.

Attempting to unify with one limited perspective of truth, whether it be a political party or a particular religion or point of view, is like thinking that just one piece of a jig-saw puzzle is the whole thing; it destroys diversity and individuality. The challenge of a puzzle is figuring out how the separate parts fit together to complete the whole picture while assuring that each part still maintains its own identity.

At times, humans so much have the urge to merge the parts into the whole that coercion is employed to force the pieces to fit. Powerful motivating forces drive the tendency to shape all the parts to conform to our view of how things should be, to convert the heathens and overthrow dictators, to convince you that my religion should be your religion. Despite the fact that existence mandates separation—two cannot become one—humans continually attempt to become gods by forcing the many into the one, and of course we all think that we are that one most important piece.

The pursuit of unity is, at times, simply a ruse to get you on my side. Religious believers try to convert the heathens, husbands and wives attempt not only to shape one another into an image of perfection, but attempt to do the same with their children, political parties work to convert the nation while slandering and attacking the opposition. The illusion caused by either/or, win/lose thinking is that identity, security, power, and importance depends on bringing the other into our realm rather than by us entering and sharing theirs. Acting like an emperor of a separate realm, the primary goal of the ego is to mold external reality into its own universe, to unite subject and object, to make you into me or, at the very least, to make you pay attention to me.

Leaders who proudly claim they are for unity really stand for separation when they serve as the great enforcers who wage wars and terrorist attacks, crusades and holocausts for the sake of unifying the world under their banner of the one correct religion or political system. Christians, Jews, and Muslims should keep in mind the words of Muhammad, who instructed his followers to tell fellow Abrahamics, "Our God and your God is one." Effective leaders manage the Polarity Paradox of separation and unity because of their awareness of the common thread that unites.

History is replete with atrocious examples of the ways autocratic individuals and groups seek to protect security and superiority by restricting the human rights of the so-called "undesirables" by changing the shape of the pieces and forcing them into place, especially into the personal realm of the autocrat. Utopias fail because the group tries to impose a new social order that replaces individual identity with a group identity. A common vision held by spiritual seekers is that of one world without borders in which there is little if any income disparity and everyone is united into one big happy group that looks the same, acts the same and thinks the same. Revolutions and utopian communities are often based on enlightened ideals of cooperation and equality, but often fail due to neglecting the role of conflict and diversity of opinion. Misguided attempts to force unity ignore the value of boundaries that actually protect individual freedom. The French Revolution of 1789, honoring liberty, equality, and fraternity, morphed into the Reign of Terror and Napoleon's quest for world domination, as did the Russian revolution of 1917 and possibly the Middle East in the 21st Century.

Nobody knows what is best for the individual better than the individual. Yes, the relative weaknesses and limitations of the individual are numerous, but these limitations can be compounded as power-hungry leaders, all with their own serious limitations, take charge of the group. There is never a perfect solution. Sadly, the situation may be no better when the group is democratically run; consider that the average unenlightened individual historically has approved of slavery, witch burning, and the persecution of heathens.

Examples of intolerance are often found in religions that expect everyone to fit into the same mold. Jesus allegedly said, "I am the way, the truth, and the light, and no one shall find the Father except by me" (John 14:6), and Paul, "If we preach a gospel other than the one we preached to you, let them be under God's curse!" (Gal. 1:8). Not to be outdone in the area of intolerance, the Quran quotes Allah as saying "And whoever disbelieves—I will grant him enjoyment for a little; then I will force him to the punishment of the Fire, and wretched is the destination" (2:126). The literalistic interpretation of such statements as these can lead to violence and persecution of nonbelievers and is instrumental in turning people away from organized religion.

It is true that, for the most part, the way of Jesus was the way of love, forgiveness, and inclusiveness. I don't believe that an enlightened person would have intended John 14:6 where Jesus says, "I am the way, the truth, and the life, no man cometh to the Father, but by me," to mean my way or the highway, my way or you are doomed because all other ways are wrong. Jesus's alleged statement must be considered in the context of the times. First-century Palestine was a time of unrest and revolt against Rome, cults of all sorts abounded, and many claimed to be the messiah who would liberate the Jews from the yoke of Roman occupation. A truth seeker could waste a lot of time stumbling around in the search for a clear path.

Jesus was like a fireman trying to rescue people from a burning building. There might be many ways to escape, but the fireman tells the desperate occupants, "I am the way, follow me and you will live!" With fires raging and not being able to find the way out because of burning, smoke-filled eyes, you'd better follow the fireman. The fireman himself is not the only way, but it is certainly easier for the panicked occupants to follow his path rather than grope around blindly for an unmarked exit.

People join fraternal organizations, political parties, and religious denominations with the positive intent to unite in truth as they see it and to gain the security, power and approval of the group. However, this attempt to unify often results in an identity with the in-group to the exclusion or demonization of the out-group. Even political independents and those who claim to be religiously tolerant often elevate themselves above those who join mainstream churches or political parties. In college, as a proud independent, I looked with disdain on the exclusiveness of the frats, but in so doing, I was perhaps even more exclusive.

Rather than destroying opposition, unity—whether organic, societal, or physical—depends on balancing repulsive and attractive forces. The atom balances positive and negative forces, planets maintain a stable orbit by balancing inward and outward forces, and the survival of human society depends on balancing selfish concerns with the Will to Unify. In a way, the two-party system that causes the much-criticized conflicts in the United States Congress is a necessary check that prevents any one side from assuming too much power.

Dogmatism and Stereotyping

The human ability to step out of time causes us to lose our place, and hence, to feel out of place in a dynamic, constantly changing universe. It is the nature of sentient beings to not only seek to understand the order of the cosmos, and how humans fit into the picture, but to actually impose order by dividing experience and things into categories. For the purpose of understanding, we attempt to stop the universal process by breaking it down into discrete pieces that can be examined, defined and categorized.

The universe "orders" and so do we. Stars are grouped into orderly galaxies, planets are grouped into solar systems and the entire cosmos operates according to the order of physics and chemistry. Humans arrange themselves not only into tribes, nations and races but manage to arrange just about everything under the sun into a zillion categories, all for the purpose of locking things into secure and orderly compartments. We even try to stop time by packaging it into little discrete pieces we call years, months, days and hours.

This categorization often leads to stereotyping and to all manner of prejudicial thinking including the feeling that the world would be better off if everyone thought and acted like us, and joined our group—though this would bother us tremendously since our perceived myth of uniqueness would disappear. Stereotyping and categorical labeling are just one aspect of an inherent, adaptive process that drives us to simplify a complex world and to impose order on the cosmos.

There is nothing wrong with stereotyping and categorical labeling per se, we all create categories that distinguish males from females, children from adults, oranges from apples, what is safe from what is dangerous and threatening. Above all, observing differences between you and me, or between your group and my group helps to define who I am.

The problem arises when the natural tendency to categorize and organize leads to stereotyping, dogmatism and prejudices which are just a lazy means of gaining security and control. Although the Polarity Paradox includes the drive for unity as well as separation, it is easier to tear things into bits and pieces and put them into separate categories than to figure out how the parts fit into the whole.

The easiest way to satisfy the desire for unity and the security of order is by identifying with the levels of organization that resemble personal identity. Safety and security is offered by wrapping people, and one's Self, into tight little compartments labeled with permanent markers such as conservative or liberal, enneagram 4 or 6, black or white, Christian or atheist. The problem is compounded by attributing the same characteristics to all group members such as all Christians are anti-gay and white people can't jump. To label is to libel.

While categorization obviously makes life safer and simpler, this security is an illusion that not only traps the creative force but gives birth to many of humankind's deepest problems such as extremism, intolerance and prejudicial thinking. The narcissistic, zero/sum belief arises that elevating the self can only come at the expense of the other, that lowering your position raises mine.

Negative stereotyping is partly derived from the ethnocentric notion that everything is defined and judged based on the perspective of one's own group. The point becomes to see my piece, which I take credit for having created, as the Super Me of all pieces, to see the category that includes my race, my religion, my thoughts, my actions, my Positions and Possessions as being the best position.

Either/or thinking results in the myth that an absolute separation exits between where I am and where everything else is. This belief leads to thinking that happiness, meaning and purpose are also in some place separate from where I find myself at this present moment, that finding the good life requires searching all over the world for the connecting pieces that include the right places, times, ideas and things. Our very identity is fractured by attaching to these disconnected Positions and Possessions.

To find where we fit in this cosmic scheme, we impossibly try to capture and freeze these pieces thus attempting to reconstruct reality by living and becoming an imaginary vision. The pieces become so important that they become not only our personal reality but can become our very identity which now must be maintained, rated, and defended. I not only think of myself as politically independent, fiscally conservative, and socially liberal, but I defend these god-points, these Positions and Possessions, by thinking they are absolute truth and I wonder why everyone doesn't believe the way of the Super Me.

New insecurities and even paranoia arise from the pressure to defend rigid categories from threats. Putting God in a box also puts *you* in a box which is understandably tempting, after all, a locked box does offer a safe way to escape the problems of the world and avoid confusing nuances. The danger here is that extreme effort is necessary to keep the lid closed and to safely defend the contents.[1] The consequence of extreme measures on one side is the activation of Newton's Third Law, For every action there is an opposite and equal reaction, as the opposition attacks in full force.

Contributing to polarized thinking and extremism is inertia's seemingly unavoidable pull that comes with any action or belief. Polarization, and hence categorization, gets us stuck on the path toward extremism by seeing in only one direction and not only ignoring any truth from the other side but failing to see the big picture.

We all know irritating people, and at times this is most certainly us, who are absolutely convinced that their perspective is the only correct way to view the world. This god-like, emotionally-based certainty ignores facts and logic and cuts off communication. The insistence that I am right and you are wrong creates an irreconcilable barrier to connection, especially when backed by religious or political dogma.

At one time or another, we are all guilty of dogmatic certainty, such as when we tend to blame everyone else for the problems

---

[1] I do have to mention that care must be taken here; some stereotyping may be nothing more than making rational associations based on past experiences.

of the world, or when a Democrat refuses to give the Republicans credit for having any positive influence, or when a sports enthusiast "hates" a certain football team. Whenever you issue the cry, "I hate that," or "No way!" or "This is the only path to salvation," it is an indication of polarized thinking that totally accepts one side, our side, while absolutely rejecting the other.

Stereotyping and over-generalizing soon allows one aspect to dominate the whole thing—one bad apple spoils the barrel. For example, political candidates are often totally rejected for making one careless statement. Just one negative detail may spoil our attitude toward an entire experience or one disagreement may poison an entire relationship. I am now writing this in a coffee shop I have never visited before. My first cup was outstanding, but my decaf refill tasted like mud. For a while, the lousy coffee upset my entire mood, but the rotten apple need not spoil the barrel. I appreciated how quiet the shop was and enjoyed watching the Olympic results on the TV. I exercised my freedom of choice to create a better mood by changing perspective. And like existence itself, my experience in the coffee shop was part of an integrated whole that was more than the sum of its parts. But next time I will choose regular coffee.

Discriminating analysis can either increase one's appreciation for the whole or obscure the big picture by splitting the whole into separate pieces. Noticing the nuances of a glass of wine, the appearance, nose, taste, and finish, can greatly enhance the tasting experience. But discrimination can be carried to an extreme. Here is one of life's many dilemmas. The more knowledge one has about, say, wine, the more aspects of the wine tasting experience can be appreciated. However, the wine connoisseur may get so carried away judging the aspects of the wine's nose and legs that the connoisseur ignores the body that includes not only the wine but the camaraderie of friends and the winery's pastoral setting. The connoisseur can easily become overly critical, with unrealistic expectations and harsh judgments that lead to an appreciation for only the most expensive wines. Too much intellectual discrimination can destroy an experience. With analysis comes the danger that the separate parts of the experience become disconnected from the whole. Appreciate the trees but also be grateful for the forest.

Then there are all those judgments that seep into the minds of intellectuals who claim to be nonjudgmental. The more positive value I place on being nonjudgmental, the more negatively I look upon those who fail to measure up to my high standards. The higher my standards are for being a responsible citizen—by voting, recycling, conserving energy, helping the unfortunate, being friendly to strangers, and so on—the more I am bothered by those who don't do these things. Can't win for losing, as the saying goes. The more highly I value being nonjudgmental, the more critical I become of my own tendency, and that of others, to render judgments.

The survival of the human race may depend on overcoming the natural inclination toward polarization and distrust of the other. Humans are blessed with the gift of the center which, by avoiding dogmatic certainty and Identifictions, allows for the recognition of common desires and purposes that integrate polarity. The rich reward for being in the place of the other is a detached perspective that provides the awareness of shared participation in this cosmic play.

Humans can change the psychological distance from which the world is viewed. The greater the distance between two objects, the more they look the same. When looking at the night sky with the naked eye, heavenly objects all look the same; we can barely tell the difference between a star, a planet, and the Andromeda galaxy with its billions of stars. When I take my daily walk to the top of the nearby hills, I can't tell whether the people on the trail far below are male or female, young or old, fat or skinny. From a distance, with differences barely noticeable, I render few judgments, and for this reason many relationships are conducted from a distance. But differences become apparent as hikers get closer, and then judgments seep in: Why is that guy wearing a sweatshirt with the hood up on such a blistering hot day? Look at that foolish girl hiking a rocky trail in flip flops. That kid just brushed against poison oak. Even closer contact, such as engaging in conversation, may reveal attitudinal differences as well, so people often keep a safe distance by talking about superficial, impersonal things, conversing in clichés and catchphrases.

Although differences are revealed as relationships grow closer, when we look really, really close, we again see similarities. If conflicts and disagreements resulting from a close, intimate relationship can be overcome, then the two become one in the mutual discovery of the universally shared authentic Self that lies beneath the defensive layers of fabricated Identifictions. However, as will be discussed later, intimacy is often avoided for fear of finding that our prized uniqueness is not as unique as we thought.

So far we have the following materialistic myths that interfere with finding the truth of Self: positions count, my position is the most important, I am separate from you, and we are all separate from God, external authority is more important than internal, high positions are better than low, and possessions count—the more things the better, and the bigger the better. The next chapter will discuss the myth that all is well and good if only the missing piece can be found.

The sage understands how a contrasting, yet dynamically balanced life is connected to overlapping levels—the particular and the universal, Self and other—and to polarities such as male and female, conservative and liberal. Interrelationships depend on the contrast between Self and other while knowing how the moral strengths of one side act to moderate the moral strengths of the other. As an example, the fiscal conservative can act as a restraint on the moral strength of the liberal's tendency to raise taxes to help the poor. Higher taxes can have the unintended consequence of actually hurting the low-wage earner by decreasing the slim profit margins of small businesses that provide most of the nation's jobs. On the other hand, if taxes are too low then inadequate revenue may cause a loss of jobs as companies and cities go bankrupt.

Conflicts that ensue from polarization are as much a part of human interactions as the inevitable cosmic conflict between dark energy and dark matter. The tug-of-war between separation and unity, between the tendency to split existence into pieces and the need to put them back together, reflects a fundamental conundrum. However, the negative consequences of dualistic thinking can be ameliorated by committing to the belief that unity embraces diversification.

Either/or thinking ignores nuances and the overlap between roles, categories and polarities—at times I am conservative, at times liberal, at times aggressive, at times nurturing. I am more trusting and less fearful of the other by recognizing that your identity and mine are free of the constricting boundaries of categories. Negative stereotyping, categorizing and hyper-partisanship can be minimized when people of different religions, races and political parties come together and first identify similarities and common goals before discussing differences.

CHAPTER 4

THE GREATEST HIGH OF ALL

The Myth of the Missing Piece

> Sobriety diminishes, discriminates, and says no: drunkenness expands, unites, and says yes. It is in fact the great exciter of the yes function in man.

—William James, *The Varieties of Religious Experience*

"Break on through to the other side." This line by The Doors alludes to the powerful desire to break down the barriers and walls of convention and role playing that separate a disconnected, dissatisfied self from the pure experience of an unfiltered, joyful reality. We want to escape the ego attachments that lead to a state of lonely, meaningless isolation that makes us too often feel apart from, rather than a part of, the sought after greater reality where reigns eternal happiness, contentment and meaning.

It seems that a force deep within screams to transcend a shallow, disconnected life, layered by transitory symbols comprised of Identifictions. This deep-seated desire is to leave behind a life empty of meaning and purpose in favor of finding the greater boundless reality of the Super Connection where there is no separation between where I am and where I want to be, where there is no separation between you and me, and where the Self is not split between subject and object.

The need to escape must be of great concern since, according to the *Guinness Book of World Records*, the word "drunk" has more than two thousand synonyms.

We want to get high all right; we want to reach into the heavens and leave behind the gravitational pull of earthly concerns that drag us down. We want to escape from the plague of dissatisfaction and the desire to acquire that drives the frustrating never-ending search for the perfect answer. Timothy Leary, the counterculture guru of the psychedelic 1960s and 1970s, popularized the phrase, "Tune in, turn on, drop out." Although Leary irresponsibly advised the youth of America to turn on with LSD, his phrase had a deeper meaning. We want to turn on the sensory system's heightened sense of pleasure and awareness, tune in and focus on harmonious unity with the Order of Cosmo, extinguish the fear of letting go, the fear of eliminating Identifictions that inhibit authenticity and prevent the full realization of the human potential for experiencing love and joy.

The desire to transcend limitation and finiteness, the urge to merge with something greater than the individual self may be an expression of a cosmic order that "wants" to reconnect with its source and a lost moment of unified singularity like a little water droplet splashed out of the ocean "wants" to return to Mother Ocean. Is there a human need to participate in the creation of something grander than the individual as the sperm seeks to unite with the egg, as atoms are attracted to one another to form molecules and as cosmic dust coalesces to form stars?

Without the tiny drops, there would be no ocean. The essence of the individual drop and the vast oceanic waters is the same; their difference is only due to position and quantity. Once in a while a few drops separate, change position, splash up from the surface, evaporate, and perhaps see their identity as being different from the ocean. The waves go up and down, tides bring water in and out, but all of the water eventually cycles back to the source.

There is no identity, no existence, no consciousness, without the one taking notice of the many and the many taking notice of the one. True identity, not to mention physical and mental health, is enhanced by recognizing the truth of the other.

At the basis of the endless quest for ever more stuff, and for ever more fame and fortune, is the quest for the answer to the core question to which all other questions relate; How do we find permanent, absolute happiness, contentment, meaning, and eternal life? Where is the perfect place to find the Absolute, where is that missing piece?

Humans spend a great deal of time and energy trying to make sense of the world; we define, organize, categorize, stereotype, generalize, break things down, look with telescopes into the far reaches of outer space and then scan inner space with electron microscopes. What we are searching for is the God Particle, that one common element from which everything is derived.

Humankind suffers the illusion that somewhere there exists a transcendent God of Perfection in the form of a thing, an object, a goal, a greater reality of absolute meaning and perfect happiness that can only be found by leaving the Self of the present, by looking for some thing out there somewhere. If only we could find that one perfect missing piece to complete the puzzle. If we could just find the right things, the right place to live, the perfect job, join the right group, find the perfect mate, adopt the right philosophy or religion, then enlightenment would be ours. But no matter what, a piece to the puzzle always seems to be missing, and we seem to always be just a little off target. We have succumbed to the Myth of the Missing Piece.

The Greatest High of All

Happiness and finding truth doesn't require any super powers or talents, there is no missing piece, no perfect place. God purposely made this whole thing very simple. It doesn't mean for us to look under every stone, or to read every book. Though every stone and every book contain the answer, there is no one special stone to turn, no one special book to read. You don't have to rely on a guru to show you the truth. There are no techniques to learn, no goals to attain or knowledge to grasp, no positions to occupy, no special churches to attend, no places to go or possessions to acquire.

So, what's the answer? Where is happiness to be found? Where is enlightenment to be found? Where am I to be found? Not in possessions, things wear out and go out of fashion. After a while, so many possessions pile up that the possessions possess the possessor. Extra shelves and storage sheds only create additional spaces that seem to always end up being filled. If only we could get away from it all, out from under the burden of the clutter, but we can't leave because we have to feed the guard dog.

The answer isn't found in positions. I have tried changing positions. I have looked to the past and future, I have been here, there, and everywhere. So what is left? Now where do I look?

These endless quests contribute little to satisfying the desire that underlies all searches, the yearning to find meaning and satisfaction in the here and now, and to be committed to the perfection of the moment, our moment. The perpetual and futile search for happiness and meaning by looking away from the moment reveals only images and symbols of the connections we seek. The consequence of believing the Myth of the Missing Piece is a nation of people who are frustrated, oversexed, over-drugged, over-fed, drowning in debt and who find themselves in a perpetual state of dissatisfaction.

Perhaps the value in pursuing this seemingly endless quest is to discover the futility of the chase and to realize that what we are questing for is really where we have been all along. As Lao Tzu said, "I can know the universe without stepping outside my house." Why travel to a Tibetan monastery only to hear the enlightened one tell you that the answer is within you, wherever you are? The gift of transcendence reveals that Truth is immanent rather than transcendent, that I don't need to do anything or go anywhere to find the contentment and meaning I am looking for, since the perfect other is the Self that I already am, in the time and place that I already occupy.

The desire for transcendence may not be to escape *from* anything, but rather to become more deeply immersed in life, to find that zone or flow. Humankind's true desire, often unrecognized, is to believe that because Cosmo is the perfect creator, so the present is perfect, and I can say, I Am the perfect creation. True transcendence, rather than an escape from the self and the world, involves a journey deep into the hidden depths of consciousness and being-in-the-world.

We have all occasionally enjoyed the exhilarating experience of feeling one with our surroundings and totally immersed in the present. This feeling of interconnectedness, that we are linked with the universal and eternal I Am of being, is the Super Connection. This feeling of oneness, the experience of unfiltered reality void of confining conventions and symbols, void of ego and selfish attachments is the epitome of the mystical and spiritual state that seems to rise above the ordinary reality of everyday life. In this sense, we are all mystics, or would like to be. The harmonious union with Cosmo allows for the discovery of the awesome truth that beauty, happiness, and meaning can be found anywhere, at any time, in the process and the product, in the mundane as well as the extraordinary.

Humankind's error is searching for the elusive needle, but ignoring the obvious haystack, or being preoccupied with the pieces while ignoring the puzzle. Self does not stand alone. The full dimension of the life experience must include awareness and appreciation of the other. There is no isolated, transcendent self just as there is no isolated, transcendent God-like supreme being, it is being itself, or rather, becoming that is the supreme process. Human beings perhaps should be referred to as human becomings.

The ultimate turn-on, the ultimate spiritual high, is when you and I profoundly connect in the mutual discovery of the spiritual awakening that comes from making the connection between Self and other. There is no more joyous, spiritual feeling than to become involved in the process of untangling the different perspectives that veil the universal truth of connections which then leads to forming connections not only with people but with nature, situations, ideas—with Cosmo, for all of these are the ultimate Other. It is the power of the force behind the Will to Unify that drives us to love and connect in sexual union.

Although getting high may not lead to the discovery of life's meaning, the drunk's quieted mind blurs differences in political or religious views, and boundaries between Self and other enough to extinguish feelings of empty isolation. For an instant, the yes function is activated. I say "Yes" to who I Am, I say "Yes" to who you are, and for this moment we both recognize the ultimate truth that Self includes other.

There is great joy and happiness to be found in discovering that there is absolutely no thing and no time in between where I am and where I want to be, that nothing is separating where you are from where I am. Wherever Cosmo is, I am, and whenever Cosmo is, I am. Open your eyes, hook up with the Great Cosmo and say yes to where you are and who you are right now for this is the greatest high.

In reality, the authentic Self, and enlightenment, is a dynamic, evolving, unlimited process that is unattached to positions, possessions, time or place. As attachments are broken, false identities along with judgments slip away. The I Am of the present has no room for false notions of the ego. I can't judge you as being more or less worthy than I am without comparing you to something in another physical location or to a past or future time frame.

The Enlightened Moment

What I really want is this moment, without past regrets or future worries. As I sit and write these words I am totally and completely accepting the world as it exists right now. But that is just part of the story; perhaps even more desired is for the world to accept me as I now exist; when you are in my presence, you represent the world to me at that moment. I want us, you and everyone, to activate the yes function and to unite with Cosmo on the same stage as we wrap our arms around each other in a mutual and uninhibited expression of affection as similarities trump differences, and in the same joyous stupor join together in the exuberant cry, "Life is fantastic here and now, you and I are fantastic, everything is already absolutely perfect!" This is the fulfillment of the Jesus Commandment to love God, Neighbor and Self, this is enlightenment. The mutual love experience of momentary perfection is the mystical oneness that unites God and human.

What we really desire is to become totally involved in experiences that are absolutely positive without such qualifications as, "I really like her, but . . . " We want to escape the jaded and cynical adult world that is filled with doubt, regret, anxiety, hesitation, mistrust and the divisive us versus them mentality — the list of things chasing us is never-ending. We want to recapture the spontaneity of the all-forgiving, all-loving child within. Is this what Jesus meant when he said be ye as children to enter the Kingdom?

The attempt to stop the flow by dwelling on the past or future, or places and things, is a futile attempt to make the infinite Self finite by transforming ephemeral images into things. Ignoring the moving process of the present causes an imitation self to become filled with comparisons and judgments and unrealistic visions of the past and future. Attachments to past memories or to future expectations become barriers to the flow of being. Enlightenment doesn't involve any kind of transcendence from the material to the spiritual, from the present to the past or future, or from human to God.

The good news is that the enlightened moment is unconditionally and unavoidably present. Truth is found on every page in the book of life, in every moment of existence. We already are what we are looking for, we just don't know it. We are the ultimate gift in disguise, we're all in the same group, I am just you from a different perspective. In Exodus, 3:14, God identified itself to Moses by saying, I Am who I Am. God didn't limit its identity by saying I am over there, or I was or I will be. God didn't go into a lengthy exposition but answered simply, as a school child might answer to roll call, by just saying, "Present."

If the present is good enough for God, it is good enough for me, for just as God is what is, so the authentic Self is what is. However, later on I will discuss the other side of the equation, the I am not since for something to exist, whether the Self or God, there must be a "not" and the "not" can be striving for goals.

The place is right now, right here in front of my nose, right under my feet. To quote Ralph Waldo Emerson, "The world globes itself in a drop of dew." The present moment is God's dwelling place as well as ours. The perfect moment for me is right now as I type these words, and the perfect moment for you is right now as you read them. The present unites Self, God and other as One. God says I Am, so I can say I Am because I Am implies You Are.

Together we share the eternal moment. It is the perfection of the moment that is the oneness where we connect with God. Keep in mind that separate conscious and physical entities must exist since unity can't exist without some thing to unify, I require you, on and off go together.

To be is to be here now, there really is no other place to be. Cosmo's "I Am" declaration is the profound statement that the absolute whatever, God, is not just being in the present but actually is the Present. If I am fully in the present, mindfully aware of what the present contains, I am being with Cosmo.

Now for a qualification that bears repeating since it is perhaps the most significant message in this book. The human tendency to capture and hold on tightly to valuables, to positions and possessions, interferes with the process of relating. The God of the I Am, the Presence, just like our Self or other selves, or enlightenment, is not a state or entity that can be defined, attained, or separated securely into a separate category, though we spend our lives trying to do just that. Existence is a continuum; the present is forever becoming the past as it slips into the future. From our perspective, limited by occupying a "place" in the cycle, the continuum is a conundrum beyond comprehension. The best we can do is to realize the authentic Self by becoming aware of how our behavior, thoughts and identity are driven by the universal conditions of existence.

We possess the ultimate prize of our deepest desires. The authentic Self is found by accepting the perfect present process as I write these words and as you read them. It is in the eternal present that dwells the authenticity of Self and other. The answers are always present in the Marvelous Mundane—if we choose to see it.

Happiness and the Marvelous Mundane

> To see a World in a Grain of Sand,
> And a Heaven in a Wild Flower,
> Hold Infinity in the palm of your hand,
> And Eternity in an hour.
> —William Blake, *Auguries of Innocence*

The truly enlightened individual—if such a person exists—seeing the connection between the spiritual and the material, experiences nirvana in the mundane by seeing the perfection of the moment. Transcending the inauthentic self of time and place gives birth to an inner vision that brings the transcendent vision of unity down to the mundane and worldly pursuits of everyday life.

The good news is that the enlightened moment is ours for the taking, right here, right now. It is not any particular place or thing, or the number or size of things, that gives us The Experience, but rather every place, every time, and every thing (or no place, no time, and no thing), *if we pay attention* and at least for a while stop multi-tasking.

Much of life consists of boring, mundane tasks: commuting, shopping, cooking, paying bills, cleaning, straightening, and organizing. Life can be pretty empty when we can't find pleasure in these activities. There is nothing intrinsically unpleasant about sorting through junk in the garage, but expectations and striving for goals take us out of the present as we think about what we would rather or should be doing.

Actually, the grass may be greener on the other side of the fence, but golden fields of grain are just as beautiful as spring wheat. As Emerson said, "The true doctrine of omnipresence is that God reappears with all his parts in every moss and cobweb." The Great Cosmo permeates every aspect of existence—the simplest ideas and the common places. It is with me as I clean up the dog's business or as I luxuriate on the beach of a tropical isle. Meaning can be found in pulling weeds or cleaning out the garage. Happiness is with us now as we experience satisfaction in completing the mundane and trivial tasks of everyday life.

The park where I take my daily walks was part of an old Spanish land grant inhabited at one time by Ohlone Indians. The other day my walking partner and I noticed sections of mud, like thin dried pancakes, scattered in the center of the trail. We entertained ourselves by trying to figure out the origins of this stuff and came to the conclusion that the rough trail jarred the mud off the underside of a truck. Another time we spotted a boulder with rather unusual holes. The holes on the side and on the top of the rock appeared to be caused by weathering, but the top holes were deeper, wider, smoother, and more uniform. We concluded that we had come upon a mortar used by the Ohlone Indians for grinding acorns into flour hundreds or perhaps thousands of years ago. We often come upon little mysteries that we attempt to solve. These are illustrations of how the common and ordinary can take on an added dimension if we are open to seeing it.

Happiness, meaning, purpose, and even ecstasy can be found almost everywhere and in everything, while watching the rain, mowing the lawn, savoring a piece of chocolate, or just sipping cold water. The Grand Canyon is awe-inspiring, but the beauty of a ravine channeled by a trickling stream can elicit wonder, as can a walk in the city. A spiritual mind doesn't require devotion to spiritual studies—the harmony of Cosmo is as available to a warrior or a garbage collector as to that of a priest.

The greatest wisdom and spiritual enlightenment is when everyday living becomes a marvelous adventure. Moving to the harmonies of the oscillating universe, as did primitive humans at the time of the emerging mind, music can penetrate being, allowing one to become the music. Beyond judgments and conceptions, we can experience the transcendent meaning of the dance and song as the rhythms, harmonies and notes become birds, wind, colors, and emotions. Freed of the influence of stifling conventions, I can find the infinite potential of my own inner being as awe inspiring as standing at the edge of the Grand Canyon.

Use the power of creation to appreciate and wonder at the beauty of Cosmo in everyday life, in everyday people and everyday things, and to see that the wonder is not in the things themselves but in Self that possesses the divine power to create absolute meaning. The wind and rain, deserts and ocean hold a wondrous beauty, but also marvel at the truth of the underlying universal form expressed in all of creation, in the branching of streams and trees, blood vessels and spider webs, in the form found in the cycles of life and death of stars, galaxies, universes and us.

Being-in-the-Zone

While grooving in the moment, two become one, lovers unite, the dancer forgets the Self and becomes the dance, the reader in the moment is transported into the story, and the Willits walker enjoys the simple beauty of the flower garden without comparing it to his own weed patch. Involvement in the eternal present defeats death and the duality that separates Self from other, or people from Cosmo. Involvement in the present gives rise to the transcendent spiritual experience when the process (creator) and the product (creation) become one. Studies have shown that this intense immersion in the moment, which psychologists refer to as "flow," and is sometimes referred to as "being-in-the-zone", is a major component of happiness. Questions relating to goals, purpose and the meaning of one's life are of little concern while a person is in the zone.

Although being-in-the-zone usually refers to athletes, it also applies to the reader who is completely absorbed in the story, the weekend gardener tilling the soil, or the stand-up comedian who is at one with the audience. Being in the zone, one is free of judgments and comparisons, and is totally absorbed in the present with no desire to be anywhere else.

The power of the present is manifested in the zone by becoming oblivious to time. Being "in the zone" is described in almost mystical terms: "Time seemed to slow down; I could see the seams on the ball; the tennis racquet felt like an extension of my arm." Often an athlete totally immersed in the game is oblivious to heat or cold or crowd noise, and may even ignore intense physical pain.

Being in the zone could be compared to what we feel when we've killed awareness of time so that it seems to fly by so fast that we're unaware of its passing. Let's say I am at a party, having a great time, in part because I am oblivious to time. In the process of losing awareness of time, of killing time so to speak, I have also lost the evaluative self that exists outside of time. Being absorbed in the activity, lost in the moment, I am feeling one with the partygoers. Then, for an instant, I step out of the party mood, thinking, "I'm having such a great time, I don't want this party to end." My evaluative self re-enters the picture, and the moment is lost. I want to be in the flow but this awareness actually stops the flow. Checking my watch, I notice that it is getting late. Now I have consciously confined the infinite flow of time with thoughts about cleaning up or where next year's party will be held, but then someone does have to clean up the mess.

Champions may become former champions because of a failing mental attitude, which is often the result of over-attachment to Positions or Possessions, time or place. Many times I have watched low-ranked tennis players win the first set against championship-caliber players only to eventually lose the match as the challenger steps out of the zone and becomes aware of playing out of "place." The challenger falls out of the moment as she measures and compares what and where she thinks she is in the rankings with where she finds herself in the match. When a lower-ranked player suddenly becomes aware of playing in the Wimbledon finals, the sudden realization may strike, "What am I doing here?" At this time, the challenger becomes attached to place, is overwhelmed by the importance of the moment, and loses the match. Spiritual seekers are often guilty as well of trying too hard to follow the right techniques for being in the moment where they already are.

The unranked challenger, figuring that there is nothing to lose, may have an advantage over the champion. No one expected the New York Giants to defeat the New England Patriots in Super Bowl XLII. David Tyree, a little known Giants wide receiver, typified the attitude of the champion in making one of the most spectacular catches in Super Bowl history. Up until the big game, the Patriots were touted as possibly the best football team ever, with their quarterback, Tom Brady, as possibly the best quarterback in history and Randy Moss as the all-time best wide receiver. For the Patriots, everything was at stake, and they had everything to lose. Being super-aware of their lofty position as the number one team, and with high expectations for victory, the Patriots may have been too attached to their status. The Giants, playing relaxed and loose with fewer expectations, figuring they had nothing to lose, became the victors.

Many years ago I was a pole vaulter. This event illustrates how being-in-the-zone reflects the art of playing Catch and Release, which will be explained in an upcoming chapter. As in many endeavors, there must first be the catch phase fueled by adrenalin and the desire to win. Mastering the pole vault requires a fast run down the runway and an aggressive pole plant, but then the vaulter must relax, rock back into position, and wait for the pole to bend during the release stage. The vaulter who tries too hard stays in the catch phase too long, tightens up, pulls too soon, and risks coming down on the cross bar. As in any endeavor, attachment and release applies to the attitude and the physical performance.

One must balance a strong desire to win with the attitude that winning isn't everything. I believe my relative success in a few championship track meets was due to the attitude I had that I was fortunate to have merely qualified for the meet and that any place I took was a bonus. Although my competitive juices still flowed, winning wasn't everything. Perhaps the belief that I was already a winner by just getting into the meet helped me to relax and defeat vaulters whose marks going into the meets were better than mine. However, there is always another side. My relaxed attitude and lower expectations, along with not stepping out of the zone to examine ways to improve my technique may have prevented me from attaining greater heights. Many of the exceptionally talented movers and shakers of the world have been obsessed with success. At times obsession has been to the benefit of civilization, at other times to the detriment, but obsessive attachment will always be at the expense of certain other connections.

Success in athletic competition or any other area is a natural consequence of playing Catch and Release. Pay attention to the demands of the present moment by releasing attachment to time and place while keeping in mind that releasing attachment doesn't mean that thoughts of winning aren't a concern.

Interrupting the Flow

I will now appear to contradict what I've said earlier. To be is to be here now, but being and existence in some way require not being here. God also had to tell Moses, though not recorded in the Bible, "I am and I am not" since there is no being without nonbeing as a contrast. Being a champion, realizing human potential whether in sports, business, the spiritual realm or any of life's endeavors, requires knowing when to disrupt the flow, when to become attached and when to let go, when to follow convention and when to break tradition to follow a new game plan.

Survival in a material world necessitates, at times, consciously stepping out of the moment to evaluate a course of action. This is the only way to invent, innovate, and evolve not only materially and technologically, but spiritually, as well. This rare gift of transcendence allows for rapid and radical evolution as we consciously escape the limitations of an animal nature restricted by material conditions. Unless someone gets off the security of the couch and does some future planning, there is no party. The process of the present includes planning for the future.

I have spent a great deal of time putting down a materialistic philosophy of self that emphasizes the importance of Positions and Possessions, and I have criticized the human tendency to interrupt the process of the moment by focusing on end products and goals in the pursuit of some nebulous and transcendent Absolute. However, life is not a zero-sum game. There is no progress without some degree of dissatisfaction with the present; striving for goals provides meaning and direction to life and remember, someone not only has to make plans for the party but someone also has to clean up the mess when the party ends.

I have said little of ethics or morality, both of which play an important role in our relations with others and the necessary examination of such standards require detaching from flow. Being-in-the-zone, experiencing flow, has nothing to do with good or evil, a Hitler can experience flow as easily as a Mother Teresa. Ethical and moral considerations require stepping out of the moment to judge and to evaluate.

Although the cost of the journey outside of Eden is the loss of harmony with nature that renders us strangers in paradise, the evolution of consciousness, and the realization of human potential requires at least temporarily severing a kinship with nature that provides a worry-free life for members of the lower animal kingdom. It is, perhaps, my personal inability to find the connection I'm looking for that compels me to get off my duff and write this book about the importance of connections.

Futile though it may be, the attempt to recapture an elusive unified paradise has contributed to the advancement of civilization in many ways. It has led to inventions, scientific and medical breakthroughs, and to the founding of corporations and nations but perhaps to the detriment of spiritual evolution. The perpetual pursuit of perfection, the quest for the unification of Self and other, is behind the power drive of politicians and corporate executives along with the unending quest for knowledge, meaning and order.

Some places are better than other places, some times are better than other times. Evolution and change are also included in God's order; old, corroded cars need replacing, as do worn-out, corrupted governments. Abusive spouses may need to be dumped, out of control kids need to be brought under control. There is a danger in going with the flow, of not stepping out of the present to evaluate—for example, normally law-abiding citizens can get caught up in the rhetoric of a demonic dictator or in the destruction of riotous protesting crowds.

Judgments are obviously essential. Survival requires splitting existence into parts and judging between alternatives. Humans can't avoid establishing boundaries, endings and beginnings that only come from stepping out of the present moment. The life part of the cycle dominates experience. Life is the reference point. We can't be so enveloped in unity consciousness that we do not see the difference between consuming string beans and strychnine.

Accepting the perfection of the Great Cosmo, the eternal I Am, can lead to some strange and dangerous thinking. Not too long ago, a very misguided and irresponsible United States senator from Indiana made the ridiculous statement in a debate that he was opposed to abortion in the case of rape, since the resulting pregnancy would be God's will. His opponent, using the same reasoning, should have retorted that the rape itself was also God's will, so why place any restrictions or punishments on rape? Yes, in a metaphysical sense, whatever happens is the result of Cosmo's perfect plan, but while how we think and what we choose may be determined and caused by many antecedents, we still must accept responsibility for our choices.

We live in the paradoxical realm where two worlds are perceived simultaneously: the world of material limitations where death and finality are real, and the unbounded world of endless possibilities and infinite experience that can't be measured. Time, the state of separation, solid material substances, and free will may be only illusions from Cosmo's perspective, but to us mere mortals, they are obviously very real.

One might say that human intelligence has evolved beyond

the rest of the animal kingdom due in part to the selective advantage of being goal-oriented. Being in the moment and accepting the perfect present doesn't mean that I should be content with forever looking out the window and rotting away from the comfort of my rocking chair, or that I shouldn't get out of the way of a rock falling toward my skull, or shouldn't dash to the rescue of the damsel in distress.

The awareness of limits and end points spurs us on to get things accomplished. With unlimited time there would be unlimited procrastination. Not much gets done without limits and deadlines imposed by time. Like everyone, at times I am often removed from the moment. I regret past mistakes, I mourn for lost friends and relatives. I also tend to look forward with great anticipation to upcoming gatherings of family and friends or to trips abroad. But at times I use the future to bring me into the moment. As the date of departure approaches for an upcoming photography trip to Tuscany, I channel my anxiety into preparing the house and yard for our absence. I straighten the house, clean the carpets, plant flowers, pull weeds, get rid of old clothes, click unsubscribe on junk mail, and reduce clutter in any number of other ways as I tackle projects long put off. The conscious awareness of time limits gives life to the present.

Being perfectly content with the present means nothing gets done, nothing new is learned, the cave isn't cleaned, the clan starves, the barbarians take over, and we forever break our backs lugging stuff around without the benefit of the wheel. Too many Americans think that enjoying the moment means spending themselves into oblivion with their Mediterranean cruises, luxury automobiles, and lavish home remodeling projects, all the while proudly proclaiming the Zen philosophy, "I live for the moment because I could die tomorrow."

Cosmo erupted with a bang, a really Big Bang of complaint at the effort of having to overcome inertia and leave the comfort of the couch to construct a universe. We like the comfort of lazying about on the couch, but it is our nature to reach out and explore the beyond. In the words of Robert Browning, "Ah, but a man's reach should exceed his grasp, or what's a heaven for?"

Just as existence may be a continually oscillating process involving expansion and contraction, separation and unity with no final end or absolute beginning, so our fundamental desire for the contentment found in the Super Connection can never be satisfied. The gift of transcendence that allows a transformative glimpse of Cosmo's order is restrained by the material illusion of ends and beginnings that is incapable of fully comprehending the infinite process. Though this dissatisfaction and judgmental nature that questions everything, moves us away from the couch, enlightenment can only be tasted by harmonizing opposition and dealing with the devil.

To be aware of separation is to be aware of limits and boundaries, not only limits of the physical body, but the limits of time. Having evolved in a material world, humans can never totally experience or understand the infinite and absolute unity of the I Am that, for some, might define God or the state of enlightenment. Is the purpose of human consciousness to provide the infinite with the experience of finiteness and separation? Total acceptance of the present and therefore, the total absence of the anxiety and dread caused by the fear of death and limit of time, may be unattainable. It is not difficult to accept the I am—it is the I am not that presents the problem. However, moments and phases of what might be considered enlightened states are experienced by all.

Being-in-Time

Our attitude toward time is weird. Since time is life, if there is anything we want more of, it is time itself, we just don't want to be aware of time's passing so we strangely talk of killing time. Now, if we are having such a great time, then obviously we want more time to continue the fun, so why don't we want to be aware of time? The answer is simply that time by itself is nothing, sort of like an empty vessel. The exquisite wine is savored while the glass is ignored. What good is a glass if there is nothing in it? You can't touch, taste, or see time. Time just has a way of passing slowly, and it bores us to death with its nothingness. In fact, nothingness is thought of as death. We have to be doing *something*, since only things have meaning, and containers, after all, are useless unless they are filled with things.

On one hand there is almost nothing more desirable than empty, unscheduled, unfilled time, but on the other hand there is almost nothing worse than the mind-numbing, boring experience of being aware of time's emptiness. We have all suffered through those sleepless nights when we wake up at two a.m. and then toss and turn for hours that drag by with mind-numbing slowness until it is finally time to get up.

As much as we'd like to become fully involved in and accepting of the present moment, and of the people and situations contained in the moment, we can't seem to avoid dwelling in the safe refuge of the past and looking into the future. We make every attempt to alter time by recapturing the past, knowing the future, and freezing the present. Attachment to whom and where we were in the past, or to where we think we will be in the future, takes us consciously out of the universal process and separates Self from Cosmo, Self from other, and Self from Self. Reveries of past love affairs not only create glamorized images of the past but prevent the full appreciation of present love.

I think a problem is that we simply take time and life experiences for granted. Don't just mindlessly go through the routine of gulping down your coffee to satisfy your caffeine addiction; feel the warmth of the cup, breathe in the aroma, pay attention to the subtle, lingering flavors. Pay attention to where you are, say yes to the present moment, for here lies the enlightened Self. If you are here, then don't desire to be elsewhere.

Become involved in your present activity. Stop, listen, and then dance to the rhythm of the falling rain. Remember, the other isn't only other people. Get out of the house, work in your yard, connect with the soil and plants. Take the initiative, walk across the street to chat with your neighbors if you can catch them in between their dash from the house to the car in the morning and from the car to the house in the evening. It is hard to love your neighbor when you don't know who your neighbor is. We may know the neighbor's hired gardener better than we know the neighbor.

Enjoying the moment includes feeling appreciative for what the moment includes. Gratitude for the moment and for the other is confirmation that the lesson of life, of existence itself, is being learned. We are grateful for the ability to participate intimately in Cosmo's rare material realm. Appreciate and wonder at awareness itself. Right now we can free our potential to create meaning, we can part the veils of convention and Identifictions that cloud the beauty of the present perfect experience.

"Thou shall not covet." The Tenth Commandment instructs us to avoid desiring that which we do not already have, and what we have is the present moment. Being here is being with the car, house, family, and body that you presently have, and to the situation in which you are presently involved. Cosmo, the Great I AM, is perfectly in the moment. But remember, the present moment, just like the authentic Self, as well as Cosmo, are not objects that can be captured; I am includes I Am Not, and someone always has to clean up the mess.

What's Your Purpose?

How can I be in the moment when society disapproves of so many moments?

There's a difference between looking *to be in* the perfect moment and looking *for* the perfect moment. Convention seems to frown on enjoying an activity just for the sake of the activity. The activity, to be socially acceptable, must have a clearly defined purpose with an end product or goal kept clearly in mind. The human mind is uncomfortable with unplanned chaos and disorder. Everything must have an appropriate time and place.

Having a defined purpose and goal, as a photographer I am provided with a socially acceptable way to spend hours appreciating and focusing on the beauty of common ordinary things, such as the grain in a piece of wood or the morning dew on spider webs. Perhaps I should always carry a camera as a ready-made excuse for taking in the beauty and wonders of creation. Running down the street is okay if the goal is to lose weight, exercise, or to win a race or to escape from the bad guys but not to run just for the fun of it. It is acceptable to frown while driving or walking, but we look twice at a person who smiles when the external stimulus for the response isn't visible. Once again, the tendency is to seek order by arranging everything into set categories, and due to a brain geared to thinking in terms of black and white, to separate the product from the process, and to look outside the Self for guidance as to what is acceptable behavior.

Notice how we react to people who trust their inner-Self by accepting the joy and meaning of the present moment. Think of what your reaction would be to seeing a solitary adult skipping merrily down the sidewalk singing and laughing. You would think this guy was crazy, and it's a sad commentary on society to say, you would probably be right. At the very least, this person would be looked at as some weird eccentric that should be kept away from children. What a sad commentary on modern society. Who are the real crazies?

We are so uptight when it comes to self-expression that talking to ourselves is frowned upon, and of course our sanity is really suspect if we answer. Think how absurd this is. Whistling alone is borderline acceptable. We can sing alone if we are careful to only sing in the shower, but talk alone, talk to ourselves—this is definitely not socially acceptable at any time.

Why is it forbidden to talk to oneself? The main purpose of talking is to communicate with others, but society seems to have a problem with people who talk to communicate with themselves. Communicating with the self by recording thoughts in a journal is entirely acceptable, yet talking to oneself is unacceptable because it seems to serve no purpose, and a process without purpose is unacceptable.

We Are All Olympians

Goals and performance standards are important but when overemphasized, the moment is lost. Objective performance standards create many illusions such as that being an athlete requires exceptional strength or speed, or that intellectual brilliance make a scholar, or that musical ability is required to be a musician. Preoccupation with performance standards kills the process. The performer now objectifies himself as he becomes concerned with proper form, the height of his jumps, and the reaction of the audience and critics who compare his performance to some arbitrary standard. By objectifying the activity instead of enjoying the process, the performer transforms the sport into a false god by ignoring the fact that the dance along with the dancer forms a connection with universal order.

I am an artist, dancer, musician, philosopher, writer, athlete, all of these and more, for infinite experience is open to all. I can enjoy swimming as much as Michael Phelps, running as much as Usain Bolt, and dancing with the exuberant passion of a Baryshnikov, and yet my form and times may be terrible, and maybe I can't jump more than a foot off the ground. All of these activities simply require an awareness of universal principles such as symmetry, balance, motion, contrast, attachment, and release along with an open mind.

Unity consciousness is the connecting of subject and object, process and product, in harmony with the natural order of Cosmo. The dancer isn't defined by the height of the jumps, rather, swinging to and fro, the dancer understands how movement involves participating in the cyclical and symmetrical balance of the cosmos. The authentic observer of the dance appreciates the natural harmonies and rhythms of being, and it makes no difference whether the dance is a ballet or an Irish jig. To dance I need only flow in harmony with the rhythms of the universe. I don't need conventional music. I can dance to the pattern of the falling rain, to the crackling of frying bacon, or to the music in my head, and even Baryshnikov couldn't have done that, for he would have needed a stage, audience, and orchestra.

Baryshnikov demands a fee; I dance with God —I dance for free.

Of course life is to be experienced as a process, but too often it is fractured into isolated goals and end products. A professional athlete's enjoyment of the sport is often limited by being overly attached to arbitrary performance goals, to an end product such as a Super Bowl championship or to an Olympic title. Have you ever enjoyed singing in the shower where your scratchy voice and off-key notes won't be judged by others? You may not be a dancer, but haven't you enjoyed swaying to the beat of a favorite song? You may not consider yourself an athlete, but don't you recall how energetically you frolicked with your children? You may not be a Shakespeare, but even the bard could not have been more involved in composing sonnets than when you poured your soul into the romantic letters penned to the one you loved. The journey and the destination, in a sense, are one and the same.

Although I often feel driven to complete this book, I must also realize the worthwhile process of writing, thinking, discussing, editing, and organizing the subject matter. I may complete this book but my involvement with these ideas will never cease. The gardener who enjoys the process of weeding, fertilizing, and pruning is more likely to produce a beautiful garden. Weight loss is a goal of many Americans, but those who really enjoy being active and eating fresh fruits and vegetables are the ones shedding the pounds. Once the ideal weight is reached, the game isn't over.

Potential to experience a full life is realized to the extent that one can connect the how, what, and why (process, product, purpose). No matter the endeavor, whether art, entertainment, business, sports, politics, sex or religion, become involved in the process. As the process unfolds, the goal takes care of itself.

Experiences are meant to be universal, not just reserved for the intellectually, musically, artistically, or physically gifted. What a shame that so many of us are reluctant to become involved in music, art or athletics simply because of the false notion that these endeavors are reserved for the talented few who meet arbitrary standards. What nonsense, what tragedy.

Use your power of creation to find your own happiness, to find your own unique purpose. To get the most out of life, Cosmo sets no arbitrary standards for strength, speed, intelligence, wealth, status, or anything else. To find happiness and meaning, there are no goals to pursue, nothing to measure, no standard of excellence to achieve, nothing to learn, and no place to go. You don't need an excuse to connect, drugs are unnecessary, a stage isn't required to dance and sing. Be open to the fact that you are in a perfect place right now. The problem arises with the failure to understand and appreciate the perfect present process. This is what is real.

CHAPTER 5

THE POWER OF CREATION

The Fear of Nothingness

The I Am is the easy part, dealing with the other side of the equation, the I Am Not, the off stage, is the challenge. But as we shall see, it is only by giving up that we find our true super power and greatest gift.

The root of all fear, the fear of the unknown, ultimately the fear of death, looms ever nearer as the security of Positions and Possessions and Identifictions fades away, but the grand prize we're after, the authentic Self, and the satisfaction and contentment of accepting the moment and feeling one with the other, requires letting go of comfortable attachments. If we don't release the barriers, we're stuck on only one side.

When we were children trembling in the dark, fearful of monsters lurking under the bed, our parents reassured us by saying, "Don't worry, there is nothing to fear, Mommy and Daddy are here." Actually, nothingness, a state empty of Positions, Possessions and Identifictions, is our very greatest fear. The deeply held fear that death is the ultimate state of having no thing, no time and no possessions gives rise to the feeling that having more of everything will naturally keep us away from our greatest fear (other than public speaking)—that of death. Nothing is worse than no things.

Being so attached to Positions and Possessions, we are unfamiliar with the quiet solitude of empty space and time. Modern humans can't stand nothingness, emptiness, being alone with nothing to do. Idleness is viewed with suspicion in nearly all cultures. Boredom, doing nothing, is a type of psychological death, in fact, nothingness is death and for this reason, retirement, with its prospect of unlimited free time, is sometimes dreaded, and vacations are often filled with so many activities that one looks forward to going back to work to catch up on some rest.

Emptiness is nothingness, and we have a mighty urge to fill up empty spaces. Empty lots need houses, empty rooms and shelves soon get filled to capacity, empty spaces on the calendar become filled with appointments, an empty mind becomes filled with concepts, images, prejudices, myths and strange notions. Empty time bothers us so much we talk of killing it. But then this desire to fill up empty space is perfectly natural. After all, Cosmo chose to fill the void with something rather than nothing.

We find many ways to fill the void. We may turn on the radio as soon as we climb into the car, or immediately turn on the TV on arriving home from work. Coffee shops are filled with people who prefer working at their laptops or checking Facebook in the midst of other bodies rather than being at home alone, even though no attempt is made to connect with other people in the shop. The company found in crowds of shoppers or festival goers or the voices of talk radio is comforting and helps to allay feelings of loneliness. Sexual intercourse offers the ultimate physical connection, especially if it is associated with a sincere love between partners, but even sex between two committed lovers isn't enough to satisfy the desire for the Super Connection.

It is our hope that having many friends and being constantly occupied with the business of daily activity will fill the void of being alone in the world. However, even the company of others may not alleviate feelings of isolation. Feeling empty and alone in the midst of crowds is a common experience.

Finding time alone becomes increasingly difficult in today's constantly connected world. Even when hiking alone in the woods or standing in line at the grocery store many people are plugged into their smartphone. One possible reason for the avoidance of spending time alone may be that an unoccupied mind seems to fill itself with negative thoughts and problems, after all, humankind evolved to be problem solvers. In our culture, solitude is also associated with being lonely, depressed or antisocial.

Perhaps a first step toward losing Identifictions is to feel comfortable in silent solitude. As a reaction to the negatives of being constantly plugged in to media, people are now beginning to see the value in solitude as meditation and different forms of mindfulness find increasing popularity in American culture. The experience of one extreme opens us to rebounding to the opposite extreme. Convincing data is literally pouring in as thousands of scientific studies show the psychological and physical benefits to meditation. It was during solitary encounters with nothingness that Jesus, Buddha, and Muhammed not only discovered their true identities but also the revelations that led to the founding of the world's major religions. The ground of being, the ultimate reality of Cosmo, only enters a mind empty of judgments, definitions and Identifictions. Sometimes, being empty-headed is desirable.

Stripped of attachment to Positions and Possessions, the false self loses definition as the walls of its separate universe are broken down. When the false self is emptied of Identifictions, boundaries between Self and other vanish as we are sucked into what seems to be a meaningless void in which all that is important has no location in time or place. The state of detachment can be lonely and frightening and can lead to deep despair causing us to cry out to God, "Show me the way!"

To fill the vacuum left by the loss of attachments to false identities, and to escape the anxiety of lonely separation, one may turn to religion, or to the dogmatic adherence to whatever or whoever provides the security of simple, definite answers such as gurus or autocrats or conspiracies, or become addicted to drugs, sex or food.

Fear of letting go is not just a fear of losing precious attachments but is also a fear of what may be discovered. Either way identity is threatened. The fear of being alone, may be the fear of encountering the authentic Self. Andre Gide, a French philosopher and recipient of the Nobel Prize for literature, said individuals have a "fear of finding oneself alone . . . and so they don't find themselves at all." We have a fear of what will be found in the far reaches of the inner-Self. Being unattached to Positions and Possessions is kind of like stumbling into a dark cave. There is fear of finding an evil dark side and of being confronted with personal failings and weaknesses. As Oscar Wilde wrote in *The Importance of Being Earnest*, "I have never met any really wicked person before. I feel rather frightened, I am so afraid he will look just like everyone else," or, I might add, just like me. The equality exposed when barriers are removed can indeed be frightening.

But a profound awareness of separation reveals a greater fear with the unveiling of the bond connecting Self with other. I would add to Gide's famous quote by saying that by not finding oneself alone, one not only fails to find the Self, one also fails to find the other. With the discovery that my truth is also the truth of the other, I find that I am linked with saints as well as sinners, and with that revelation comes the fear of the awesome responsibility and power of the knowledge of Love.

A leap of faith is required to lose attachments to false identities, to the Identifictions that have been lived with for so long–perhaps a leap of faith should be called the leap of doubt. It takes faith to believe that something worthwhile will come from great personal sacrifice. Before I leap into the unknown chasm of nothingness, I want to make sure that something will be there to catch me. But since the reality is that personal identity often rests on a false foundation of ghostly images, there already is nothing holding us up. The clothes we wear, the physical appearance we carry around, the house we live in, the car we drive, the job we hold, even our ideologies are all excess baggage burdening us with false images of who we really are.

If we weren't afraid of nothing, we wouldn't be afraid of anything. All fears would be conquered if it were possible to really understand the profound spiritual truth that to give is to gain. In other words, the way to lose fear, even the fear of death, is to lose attachments (hang-ups) — the greater the attachment, the greater the fear. It is perhaps our mission to understand this. But good luck in doing this, as captives of a material world dominated by space/time, to one degree or another, attachments are here to stay. And knowing that matter comprises no more than five percent of the known universe is not much help in overcoming attachments to the precious stuff.

Understand that we are free to change perspective and to see absolute meaning in the present moment. It is the limiting position of place that prevents the experience of the infinite. We see death as a thing occupying the end position of time, but we can confront death, our most basic fear, by losing attachment to Positions and Possessions, to place and time. When we lose attachment to Positions and Possessions, we lose the foundational identity as separate beings, the inauthentic Identifictions that separate Self from other. By living in the eternal present, end points cease to exist and death loses value. If death has no value, it of course has no meaning. To be totally in the eternal present is to defeat death.

Humans, as a product and process of the universe, experience what the universe experiences. In many ways, we share in the pain and conflict of giving birth to the new; a mother suffers pain in child birth, the United States erupted in the painful Civil War before giving the slaves a new birth of freedom, as did the colonies during the American Revolution and as the Middle East suffered in the violent disruptions of the Arab Spring. The death of millions as a result of the Black Death during the Middle Ages led to the chaos and destruction of the old feudal order but contributed to the birth of the Renaissance. We have all heard stories of people in the depths of depression and despair suddenly turning their lives around and perhaps the most profound symbol of death giving birth to life and that to give is to receive is found in the Christian tradition of the death and resurrection of Jesus which offers the hope that ends are balanced by new beginnings.

The Deathly Fear of Letting Go

Wow, are we afraid to let go, to lose control. Giving up things, losing attachments, is a metaphor for death. No one wants to be a loser. We have a hard time giving things away. We want to be on top of the heap with as many toys as possible. Don't we want to be fulfilled? We want our coffers filled with unlimited amounts of fame, fortune and fun, beauty and brains. Personal identity seems to slip away when Positions and Possessions are lost.

The desire to give certainly isn't as strong as the desire to acquire. The feeling associated with giving a box of old clothes to Goodwill may not compare with the high of the buy that comes with the purchase of that flashy new car. The nervous system is designed to experience pleasure only by receiving external stimulation. Eating chocolate is certainly more pleasurable than giving chocolates away, and receiving a back rub is more pleasurable than giving one.

The hesitation in giving things away is based on the myth that happiness, meaning, identity and survival itself depend on external conditions and things that must be acquired, just as religions consider God to be external and separate from the I Am of personal experience. And after all, it's pretty obvious that the food we eat and the air we breathe are outside things that must be taken in.

Losers Are Winners

It is great being a loser. Losers are freed from so many worries. For one thing, there is only one way to go when you are on the bottom, and that is up. Things can only get better. Without possessions or attachments, you don't have to worry about losing anything. If I am poor, I don't have to worry about losing wealth. If I have no money, I escape the tax man. If I am ugly, I don't worry about losing my good looks. As a personal example, now that I am bald, I am free of at least one attachment. I am no longer bothered by the wind messing up my hair. I spend no time grooming, never worry about forgetting my comb, it takes my wife ten seconds to cut my hair. I laugh when I see ads for hair restoration products. Why would I want to go back to all the fuss and bother of having a full head of hair? In the words of Janis Joplin, "Freedom is having nothing left to lose."

But it really never was the hair that was the problem; rather, it was my (conscious) attachment to it. With or without my hair, I am the same person. Losing attachments doesn't mean that toys are thrown away, only that losing them won't be such a big deal.

Jesus profoundly understood the principle of losing to win and how attachments break the divine connection. The disciples were instructed to give up their possessions and follow him. "Whoever of you does not renounce all that he has cannot be my disciple" (Luke 14:33). "It is more blessed to give than to receive" (Acts 20:35). In Luke 14:26, when Jesus told his followers to hate their parents and even their own lives, he was using an extreme example to point out that all attachments, even our attachment to what we love most, can interfere with humankind's mission to reunite with God. And of course we know the important role sacrifice and martyrdom play in many religions since the ultimate detachment is from life itself.

Another great advantage of being a loser is that everyone around you becomes a winner. And when everyone around you is a winner, then so are you. And what must we lose? Primarily, we must lose the feeling of special self-importance and the false identities with Positions and Possessions, fame and fortune, for these are the Identifictions that obscure the authentic Self.

The rich and famous super-winners may be admired, but their positions of imagined superiority are often impediments to spiritual and personal growth. Humility, sincerity, honesty, and openness may be elusive qualities for the super-winner who assumes too much credit for good fortune and who personally identifies with Positions and Possessions. Humility gives birth to most virtues. Being filled up with self-importance and selfish concerns leaves no room for others. Only by accepting the

Equality of Selves can the worth of the other be accepted.

Being so caught up in the material world, we sometimes associate giving up possessions with giving away the Self and even life itself. The good news is that it is not necessarily anything material that needs to be given away. Having all the possessions in the world will not prevent you from reaching enlightenment so you can keep your money and your toys, because they have nothing to do with the authentic Self; it is the false ego-self and the ego attachment to possessions that must be given up. Attention to and interest in others is what releases self-centeredness.

Although lasting happiness and contentment may be unrelated to material well-being, to Positions or Possessions, neither is the answer found by completely annihilating desires and attachments in the pursuit of unity. Turned-on, super-spiritual gurus are often portrayed as being so detached that they are almost completely void of emotion or personality. A state of being completely detached may be free from the pain of loss, but it will experience no pleasure.

The desire for material things or sensual pleasures is so deeply ingrained that it would do little good to try to give up these things. If you have the space and the money, then go ahead and indulge yourself; no reason to feel guilty for having fun with toys. There is nothing inherently unspiritual about owning and enjoying possessions. Having a gorgeous face, a beautiful head of hair, or a fancy car is not the problem. The disconnect is caused by attachment to the idea that happiness and personal identity depends on things. The false notion that happiness depends on Positions and Possessions leads to the possessions possessing us.

Always, when one thing is lost, something else is gained, and conversely, when something is gained, something else is lost. Lessons on losing to win can be learned from every aspect of existence, from the creation of the universe to the formation of molecular bonds (size doesn't matter). In the process of giving birth to the stars and the universe, the singularity that preceded the Big Bang lost its unified state of pure energy but gained diversity in the formation of matter.

What I am about to say is admittedly pretty far out and speculative but the metaphor is a useful illustration. Actions follow thoughts is another way of interpreting Rene Descartes' philosophical proposition, I think, therefore I am. The idea of the game comes first, then the game is played. God, the Great Cosmo, had the "idea" of releasing singular identity before setting off the Big Bang. To fully express its nature, God, or the cosmic creative force, gave birth to the "experience" of diversity. To gain experience and to realize complete identity, it gave up singularity, or oneness. It is a useful metaphor to think that, in a sense, God died by sacrificing its unified oneness but its full actualization is gained through the experience of diversity.

With the death of singularity, God experiences humankind, by sacrificing self-interest and self-absorption, by transcending the illusion of isolation, by dying to the ego-self, humankind expands to find God and a greater Self. Both the universe (God?) and human seek transcendence as each seeks the experience of the other. Neither Cosmo nor human can fully realize identity without each side being willing to momentarily give up the idea of an isolated self. The cyclical nature of existence suggests that this reciprocity involving unity and diversity, losing and gaining, ends and beginnings, Self becoming other, is an infinite universal process.

Be a loser. Whether you are involved in the creative arts, sports, business, politics, being a parent, or just trying to be a friend, be a loser and you will find success. Lose the desperate drive to win at all cost, lose the feeling that you are special because the other is less special, lose the idea that you are your Positions and Possessions. Gain the understanding that you are special because the other is equally special. Gain the understanding that perfection is the authentic Self within.

Humankind's cosmic purpose may be to give God, or existence, the experience of limitation and the fear of death and non-being. Remember, the infinite must include at least the experience of non-existence, the I Am Not, and this is what humans do. The infinite subjective I Am must experience what it's like to not be God. In the process of losing momentary attachments to identity, God and human each experiences the other, God gains the human experience of finitude and the human gains God experience of the infinite; in the process of losing identity, the realization is gained that the other is of equal value, that the existence of Self requires the existence of other. For our entire lives we have been conditioned to acquire more of everything, to protect what we have, but now, with the release of the greatest attachment, the attachment to Identifictions, inner peace is found allowing for the identification of Self with other.

Gifts of the Empty Center

You might ask, "What is left of personal identity if I give up the security of the empirical ego's protective boundaries and attachments to Identifictions? If I am not a man, not a teacher, not an American, if I am not bound to one side or the other then who and what am I?" This encounter with nothingness confronts the traveler with the stark and frightening reality of standing alone, insignificant and threatened by nonexistence. However, detachment presents the opportunity to take advantage of the gifts of the center zone and it is here that one finds the true, authentic Self.

Centered in a quiet zone, void of positions and possessions, detached from extremes and desires to acquire more of everything, one discovers the inner peace of ego release. Breaking down boundaries formed by false identities allow the enlightened Self to soar free of attachments. The center is the locus of pure awareness out of which can be found happiness and joy and meaning.

Feelings and instincts often lead us astray. An ego threatened by a perceived insult lashes out at the threat, or runs and hides. But humans are fortunate to have an innate ability to escape the emotional restraints of the ego by consciously stepping outside of the experience to bracket and objectively examine negative feelings. This ability to examine the world for what it is, to reflect on experience, is what existentialists call the "phenomenological epoché," or bracketing.

We can, as the philosopher Eugen Fink says in his description of the epoché, perform the "philosophical unchaining, the tearing free from the power of one's naïve submission to the world." And to quote Rollo May, "We can't help what happens, but only what attitude we take toward what happens. In taking an attitude toward what happens we change what happens."

The center brings us as near as humanly possible to the divine experience of oneness as we find that being nothing opens the door to being everything. Standing in the center, I can see in all directions. St. Augustine said that God is a circle whose center is everywhere and its circumference nowhere. The enlightened center, the authentic Self, like the Great Cosmo, is infinite and therefore ineffable, beyond the limits of language and concepts, for it is neither here nor there, occupying no past or future. It is none of these and all of these.

The centered Self, positioned dynamically between opposites, is analogous to the mathematical concept of zero. Zero, being a place holder, is positioned between positive and negative numbers, and though having no numerical value of its own, is the source of infinite numbers. Similarly, the center is not some kind of empty nothingness. Just as the universe sprang from the silence of no time and no place, so the infinite ground of being emerges from the void of silence. As stated in the ancient Chinese Taoist text, the Tao Ching, being itself is the product of nonbeing. Just as everything we know came out of the so-called "nothing" before the Big Bang, we really can't call the center empty since out of this "nothingness" of the center emerges Cosmo's greatest power, the power of creation.

Out of the centered Self emerges the authentic love that allows the Jesus commandments to be fulfilled to love God, Neighbor, and Self. The Golden Rule, a central theme of all great spiritual traditions, is now practiced as one steps out of the false self of Identifictions to find immortality with the profound realization that Self is other. Here is found the connection between pure objectivity and pure subjectivity that frees the love that "binds everything together in perfect harmony" (Colossians 3:14).

I like to think of myself as a centrist, a middle-of-the-roader, free of attachments to ideology and extremes. What I forget is that I limit my identity by thinking of the center as a still point or a position. The center is a dynamic, constantly shifting fulcrum just as to maintain balance a tightrope walker must shift weight from one side to the other. The center depends on knowing the extremes; without extremes, there would be nothing to be in the center of. Knowing the extremes does at times require choosing to contact the extremes.

An identity detached from Positions and Possessions allows for an open-minded and rational assessment of both sides. However, the blessing of open-mindedness can result in the confusion and indecision created by the freedom to see the value of both sides but being able to participate in only one side at a time. The dilemma is like the rabbi who is asked to settle a dispute between two opposing sides. After listening to one side's argument, the rabbi declares, "You're right!" After listening to the other side's argument the rabbi nods and says, "You're right, too." His exasperated wife observes, "Rabbi, this is absurd! They can't both be right!" The rabbi sighs and replies sadly, "You're also right."

The centered person may appear to have no position, to be some empty-headed, wishy-washy individual without convictions or principles. Quite the contrary. Jesus certainly demonstrated strong convictions when, in a display of righteous anger, he threw the money changers out of the temple. Freed from the burden of tradition, dogma, and ideology, the center frees the creative mind to clearly respond to the demands of the moment and to the dictates of an unburdened conscience. This clear vision was demonstrated by Jesus's healing on the Sabbath, which was contrary to Jewish tradition.

The mind must constantly change perspective by continually attaching and detaching as the game of Catch and Release is played out in a shifting from one pole to the other. A centered person moves between the pole of activity to the pole of quiet, from a state of oneness to a state of separation and back again. The centered position allows the freedom to journey from Self to other, from the creative progressivism of the liberal to the cautious restraint of the conservative, from the cold analytical mind of the scientist to the magical realm of the mystic.

The wonderful richness found in universal connection can only result from an actualized mind that understands the experience of extremes but returns to the stabilizing force of the center. Only this mind is capable of Shiva's dance that resolves the paradox of Self and other by dealing with the devil and dancing with God.

The center can be experienced in the midst of great activity. The detached state of nothingness can be experienced by a politician in the midst of a debate, or a teacher or scientist who readily admits when he or she doesn't have an answer, or when that same person can admit to being wrong. I am experiencing this sort of detached state of nothingness when I find myself in some undesirable social gathering that I am sure is going to result in a deadly bout of boredom, yet I manage to lose my desires and preconceived notions and become happily engaged in the conversation and goings-on of the moment.

The cold, hard reality is that trying to find and maintain the center is like trying to find the balancing point between two poles of a magnet that eventually pulls you to one side or the other. While pure objectivity is a worthy goal, because rendering judgements and choosing sides is unavoidable, the centered position will always be tinged by bias.

The Power of Creation

Freed of polarity, the Self of the Center, like the Hindu God Shiva, is a creator and destroyer, the source of life and death, good and evil, love and hate. From the centered Self emerges the power of creation, the most precious gift of all, the power to grant or deny absolute value.

Meaning and significance is found as the desires for transitory pleasures are quelled. Humans naturally desire connection with something that is permanent and absolute, and for this reason the center is feared since the center itself is empty of meaning. But it is the center's very emptiness that is the source of all meaning. The center allows us the freedom to attribute absolute meaning to whatever we choose.

It is not the power of magic that humankind desires, changing lead into gold, or walking on water, nor is it fame or fortune that is truly sought. Out of the void created from the loss of attachments is unleashed God's greatest power and the true object of man's desire—the power to do the impossible which is to create something from nothing, to create meaning out of the meaningless, to impose form and order on chaos. Possessing the greatest power of all, I am now free to find meaning anywhere; I can transform sadness into happiness, I can see the marvelous in the mundane as I erase negativity by attributing value to what others view as worthless. The freedom of choice, the ability to choose from a universe of limitless possibilities, and the freedom to grant absolute value to whatever we choose puts us in touch with the infinite.

What am I left with, standing separate in the lonely center of extremes, empty of attachments to Identifictions? When all is released, the dark state of nothingness is illuminated by the truth of the always-present perfect moment from which arises the freedom to create absolute meaning. Yes, there remains a lingering fear of letting go, of losing control, and the fear of losing place. And yes, free choice increases anxiety, and trouble arises from the value judgments that necessarily accompany choices, but choice also provides a way out.

When I make a big deal out of nothing, my wife tells me, "Hey, you're making a mountain out of a mole hill." But as usual, we have things backward—the ability to make a big deal out of nothing is exactly the power we want. Humankind wants what God has: absolute power and control, universal knowledge, and eternal life. But what is coveted most of all is God's greatest attribute, the power of creation, to make a big deal out of nothing.

We often wrestle with the attempt to make nothing out of something. After many years of living in our house, we have accumulated an awful lot of stuff. We would love to downsize, but it is just so hard to part with some things that are associated with so many wonderful memories, and some stuff does have monetary value. My task here is to make nothing out of something. Once value has been given to something, it is not easy to take it away. We are all artists, our creation being value, but upon completion of the creation, the artist is likely to become proudly attached to the finished product and this attachment can lead to a host of problems. Remember, losers can be winners.

The Power of Creation allows us to view ourselves as winners or losers. Some "losers" see themselves more as victors than do the winners themselves. One of my greatest personal triumphs in high school was when I lost a high jump competition in the league finals—only I didn't think of myself as a loser. Although I had placed second, I felt like I had just won the Olympic championship. I never imagined that I would even qualify for the finals, let alone win the silver medal.

In a way, we can be winners all the time; it depends on how you look at winning. Celebrate the small, everyday victories. Maybe I have a few mundane chores to run, but in the process of driving to the store I make three green lights in a row, and that is cause for celebration. In preparation for our Super Bowl party, we cleaned off a desk that had been cluttered for eons. This morning I used my French press to brew an unusually great cup of coffee, and I celebrated. Whether I view myself as a winner or loser depends on attitude and perspective rather than circumstance.

A human is a goal-oriented creature who wants to be God, or at least desires the powers only a god would possess. But we don't have to match the accomplishments of a Gandhi or an Einstein since the feeling of satisfaction at having completed a worthwhile task can be gained simply by cleaning out the closet. We can find meaning by overthrowing autocratic regimes, discovering a cure for cancer, or simply by being a good friend who brings a smile to people or who cares for an elderly parent. As I look out the window I have a great feeling of accomplishment after having removed ivy from the fence. A goal doesn't have to be earthshaking, nor must its importance be recognized by others, as long as there is something to work toward, some condition to improve. As Alan Watts, the Zen philosopher said, "The object is not to reach any particular stage; it is to find the right attitude of mind in whatever stage one happens to be."

The inauthentic search for meaning never brings lasting satisfaction, since the insatiable hunger for fame, fortune, power and absolute purpose is based on the false premise that all of these depend on finding the perfect Position or Possession. I alone possess the power to create value. The power of creation comes from within, not without.

Creative power is often abused by choosing to dwell in a quagmire of negativity that causes sleep deprivation, worry, depression, and high blood pressure. All too often the power of creation is used to create negatives out of positives. Do we ever criticize. It is a fact that, to a certain extent, looking to see who we are requires looking to see who we are not, and identifying what is right requires recognizing what is wrong. But it is so easy to fall prey to the tendency to demonize the other rather than seeing the other as necessary for self-definition and as a reflection of parts of us. The tendency to criticize and see the negative is often a mindless habit that constantly eats away at the beauty and wonder that life offers in each moment. We miss the momentous moment by always looking for something better and by seeking the stamp of society's approval.

I recently returned from a Rhine River cruise that wound through parts of Germany and Austria and offered glorious views of ancient castles and monasteries at every turn. Expectations on a luxury cruise like this are through the roof. On the last night of the cruise, I had the misfortune of sitting across from one of the unhappiest people I have ever met. However, as she poured out her litany of complaints, I had to agree with her on nearly every point. It rained almost every day; the observation deck was often closed for viewing due to a high water level and low bridges; sleep was often interrupted as the ship clanked and groaned through lock after lock; dinner service was abysmally slow; turnips, beets, and potatoes got tiresome; and on and on. I asked her, "If I agree with every one of your complaints, then why am I so happy?" to which she replied, "Because you're confused." I then asked her, only half in jest, "What's worse, to be confused or to be unhappy and miserable?" Without hesitation she replied, "To be confused, because at least I know where I stand. I have no doubts about how I feel, and I have high standards and expectations." This miserable woman at least felt secure in her sad identity with her place in misery. I then told Ms. Miserable that this whole cruise was a joke and she wholeheartedly agreed. I then asked her, "How do you respond to a good joke?" And for an instant, as her perspective changed, along with her attachment to place, she laughed. Ms. Miserable was able to loosen her identification with misery. For a while, as she momentarily lost her place, we both had a great laugh.

This unhappy traveler and I had the same food and saw the same towns, but our expectations and perspectives were entirely different. A happy and meaningful life is ours if we choose to see at least some of the perfection of the moment. I got soaked in the rain, but the glassy-slick cobblestones glistened beautifully in the filtered sunlight, and the rain chased me into a quaint old tavern where I enjoyed a German beer and pretzel with the locals. The slow dinner service gave us a chance to become better acquainted with table companions. Rigid expectations and limited perspective stifle creativity and authenticity and so often get in the way of happiness. The unhappy cruiser expected constantly warm and sunny days, gourmet food, and to be treated like royalty, but the symbolic nature of ideas, expectations, and desires never matches the reality of the situation. The connection is the perfection. However, I can not emphasize enough the importance of realizing that it is actually the *process of connecting* that is more important that the objective connection. And it is all a matter of perspective, and we possess the infinite potential to change perspective at any time to find the perfection.

The power of creation enables us to change perspective at any time. If you are bothered that the glass is half empty or that your life is half over, then see it as half full. Former president Ronald Reagan illustrated this point by telling the story of a little girl who was confronted with the unpleasant task of cleaning mounds of horse manure out of a stable. Rather than balking at the task, the little girl joyfully exclaimed that she knew that somewhere under all that manure was a pony.

Eliminate the false idea that happiness and meaning are conditional. Studies on happiness by Edward Diener, a psychologist at the University of Illinois, surprisingly found that the chronically ill and disabled actually reported a slightly higher sense of well-being than the population in general. Happiness has been thoroughly studied, and the results have indicated that, although there is a genetic component and fundamental needs must be met, conditions such as fame, fortune, and where you live have little influence on happiness. The ill or disabled may discover the truth that happiness is unconditional and independent of where one is, what one does, or what one has.

Enlightenment, happiness, meaning and purpose is available right now. Cosmo is no more here than there. I'm reminded of a story about a Buddhist monk who was asked, while hoeing his garden, what he would do if he knew the world were going to end tomorrow. His enlightened response was, "I would continue hoeing."

I know this is a cliché, but it does help to look for the silver lining. With a little shift in perspective, we can see that many others face far greater problems. Being deaf, I can no longer be lulled to sleep by the rhythm of the falling rain, yet neither am I awakened in the middle of the night by the wind and howling coyotes. By shutting off my hearing aids, I can block out the kid who has been screaming for the last three hours of my flight back home or the roar of the snore from the man sitting next to me. With my poor eyesight, I no longer am bothered by a little dust on the furniture. Enjoy the game, step back a little, gain a new perspective, and see the humor.

We are all artists, but a very different sort than those we usually think of, for I am at the same time a creator and my own creation. I create, I live and laugh and love, and then I give my creation meaning and value. The creator and the creation are one and the same. This would have to be the case if the universe—or God—is infinite and includes all possibilities. Perspective changes as God plays Catch and Release with itself, assuming the dual roles of the other, the creation, and the Self as the creator. We happen when God lets go, God happens when we let go.

If we are free to create the happiness, purpose and meaning that we so desperately want, then why don't we do it? Why do we choose to dwell so often on the negative? Above all else, don't we want to be happy, to see the value in our lives?

The primary reason for this negativity bias, as it is called by psychologists, is that it had survival value for early humans, who had to be constantly on the alert for predators. According to neuropsychologist Rick Hanson, author of *Hardwiring Happiness: The New Brain Science of Contentment, Calm, and Confidence,* human brains are still hardwired to pay more attention to the negative. One study found that 74 percent of the words in the English language that describe personality traits are negative. But there is more to the human preoccupation with the negative that will be discussed in the chapter, Play With the Devil.

Blind to our interconnectedness, we think we have little in common with the Great Cosmo, so we are misled into doubting that we have the power to grant absolute importance to our choices. We just can't believe that the source of happiness and meaning is within our power to experience at any moment.

How easy it is to change perspective and find happiness and contentment where sadness and discontentment once reigned. This can be done in every area of our lives. As a teacher, I often became exasperated with the terrible behavior of some junior high students. To maintain my sanity when some students would give me a bad time, I would focus on the many friendly, well-behaved students, walking up to one and saying something positive. Yesterday circumstances prevented me from taking my wife on an excursion we had planned, so instead we enjoyed a gourmet lunch at home accompanied by a glass of wine, watched a video, and still made the time very special.

Trust in yourself, recognize your power of creation. Don't be imprisoned by the past or restricted by societal expectations and false notions about who you are or by what is worthwhile. You create your own reality. Your Positions and Possessions have only as much or as little importance as you place on them.

To a certain extent we are in control of our own evolution. We can counter the negativity bias inherent in our stone-age brain. Thinking positive thoughts can actually trigger changes in the brain that make it easier to have more positive feelings. Recent findings in the new science of neuroplasticity has overturned the belief held by neuroscientists for most of the twentieth century that brain structure is resistant to change after a critical period in a child's development. Numerous studies have shown that thinking, learning, and acting actually change the brain's anatomy and physiology, which is now thought to be highly pliable and moldable.

We can think of our inherent negativity bias as one expression of the devil within. But this devil can be joked and played with and transmuted into a positive form. A friend of mine jokes that whenever we're really mad at someone or something, instead of saying, "Fuck you, buddy!" we should say, "Love you, buddy!"

Choose to be happy and thankful for life and for the good things that life has to offer, notice similarities rather than differences, see the glass as being half full. Luxuriate in feelings of gratitude for those special people in your life, bask in the warmth of their smile. When something good happens take a little time to dwell in the positive feeling. This sounds like a cliché, but it isn't.

Sharing appreciation compounds the good feeling, especially when expressing gratitude for kindness shown by others. Sharing gratitude strengthens relationships, and relationships are the strongest predictors of happiness and coping with stress, according to Robert Emmons. Another gratitude researcher, Dr. Michael McCullough of the University of Miami, says that gratitude is the emotion of friendship. Savor the feeling of accomplishment after completing a task. Allow your body and soul to be permeated and enveloped by the appreciative spirit. Have an appreciative spirit as an undercurrent to your everyday activities and thoughts. Feel appreciation as both an emotion and as an intellectual concept.

CHAPTER 6

GOD'S DANCE OF CATCH AND RELEASE

Don't Get Too Close

Intimacy can be scary. Unity is a threat to individual identity. Although humankind is inexorably drawn toward connecting with the other since subject requires object, I take pride in my uniqueness.

This precious, distinct identity can be threatened either physically or psychologically if you get too close to my personal space. I fear that if you are too much like me and get too close, then I will lose the security of my place, and if I lose where I am, if I lose my positioned self, I won't know who I am. If you are not in your place, I can't find my place, so I need you as a reference point, I need a not-self in the form of an other to define who I am just as existence depends on nonexistence, God needs the devil, and something needs nothing. Even a Buddhist monk in the deepest meditative state of pure awareness, meditating on absolutely nothing, has used that awareness to transform nothingness into an objective something. If nothing is necessary for something, then nothing becomes something.

If the boundary door between Self and other is opened too wide, and as I delve into the depths of your being, I may find to my horror that my truth is also your truth which means that you and I are equals. If you and I are equal, if we are both in the same place then I lose the value of my uniqueness. With the loss of the safety of the wall that protects my separation I make the terrifying discovery that this Equality of Selves poses the greatest threat of all. We recoil from such intimate relationships—intimacy and the infinite are truly frightening. In fact, unbounded and intimate associations with the divine are considered a mark of insanity.

It is the nature of life forms to instinctively fight to preserve separation. Without boundaries to separate one thing from another there is no individual existence—to be only one thing is to be nothing.

Unity without differentiation degrades reality into a meaningless, boring, amorphous void of nothingness. Separation must be maintained, otherwise there is no object of affection, only a subject. Love is a connection, and without a separation between things there is nothing to love, nothing to unify. Unity depends on separation, there would be no coin without two sides, just as a magnet requires the connection of a north and south pole.

The Polarity Paradox is the ever-present human dilemma that surfaces in the search for the safety and security of a walled-in personal identity while simultaneously wanting the protection and companionship found in connections with the other. Caught in the obvious state of separation, we feel out of place, insecure, and alone in a cold, unfeeling and seemingly meaningless universe. Torn by conflicting desires, we are simultaneously terrified of both being and non-being, afraid of being alone and separate but also afraid of losing freedom and individuality by getting lost in the crowd. Both unity and separation are feared and loved at the same time. Now the true meaning of Hamlet's soliloquy becomes clear, To be or not to be, that is the question.

The game of life, like many games, is divided into sides with winners and losers, rules and boundaries. There is no game if there is only one side or if only one side gets the ball. To some extent, I'm afraid there will always be an Us and Them. However, it doesn't always have to be so much an Us versus Them.

Just as similar poles of a magnet repel each other so a repelling force may come into play as Self and other become intimate. The more similar two people are, the more likely that intimacy may result in one or both partners seeking ways to emphasize their differences. Intimate relationships often give rise to conflict as freedom, individuality and identity become threatened. Intimate associations between husbands and wives, parents and children, friends, siblings, and business colleagues often result in unpleasant and even violent confrontations—one in three women who are victims of homicide are killed by former or current lovers or partners and according to a 2009 All-state Foundation National Poll, 33% of all police time is spent responding to domestic disturbance calls.

The unfortunate myth of the Super Me is that Self can only exist to the exclusion of other. This myth subscribes to the polarized belief in the exclusive value of one self—my self—which holds that absolutely accepting you means that my value is diminished. As perceived by the inauthentic self, to the extent that you gain value, I lose value. I am faced with the existential dilemma as to whether there can be two absolute truths, two gods existing simultaneously in the same place, so one of us will either have to go or you will have to join my tribe.

We fail to accept the truth and value of the other in part due to a dualistic brain that divides a unified cosmos into separate compartments and perceives the self as a separate entity, a separate universe isolated from the other. We think either something exists or it doesn't, something is either absolutely true or false, I am who I am, and you are who you are, and never the twain shall meet. The problem is that, rather than looking for ways to integrate opposition, our primordial survival instinct rejects the opposition.

Self-identity, knowing who I am, is easier if the dividing line between Self and other is distinct; Once the wall is constructed, we are reluctant to let it down, and once we have something in our possession, especially personal identity, we are reluctant to let go. The more differences we find, the stronger the artificial walls become as our separate identity pushes us yet farther away from the other.

A basic law of matter is that two pieces of matter can't exist in the same place at the same time, yet because material dominates our world, the feeling is that this law is contradicted if you and I have equal value. And because of the tendency to generalize, we think this law also applies to ideas and concepts. The feeling is that the more credit I give to your idea, the more my opinion is crowded out.

Intuitively we know that we are equal in the eyes of Cosmo but we're going to identify some difference that separates us, that puts me just a little bit above others. There is only enough room on top of the mountain for me. When thinking of a best friend we may say, "Oh yeah, Ted is my best friend, really love and admire the guy, so smart, so talented, so friendly." However, we really want to add, "But let me tell you what bugs me about Ted and what his problem is, and how he is really different from me."

If our Self is shared, I not only see what I thought were my unique strengths reflected in you, but the weaknesses I may have once criticized in you become mine as well. Unity may reveal that my position is not superior to yours, and, admit it or not, we all like to think our position is just a little higher.

The myth continues. I know that I exist and that my existence is good. I have positive values, I don't litter, I return lost wallets, I am loyal to my wife, I vote for all the right people; basically, I'm a great guy. The speed I drive is the speed everyone should drive. Okay, due to a few conditions beyond my control, I made a few wrong choices, especially buying stocks at the market peak. But I am not so sure that all of these great attributes can be said about you.

The physical and psychological distance between Self and other now grants a position of imagined superiority from which one can look down on the defects of others. It's trouble enough that all of our possessions need to be protected but maintaining this imagined position of superiority requires building even more elaborate walls of defense mechanisms, both psychological and physical, and this can give rise to a host of problems including stereotypes, dogmatism, prejudice, superiority complexes, and bullying.

Seeking superior fame, fortune, and power has led to many of the wonders of modern civilization. but we will have a richer, more meaningful, and happier life, and civilizations will thrive in the long run, by opening up to the other.

Catch and Release

How can we lose the fear of intimacy, the fear that once we leave the security of the positioned self, we won't be able to come back? This fear of losing position is based on the misconception that if I agree with any part of your position, my own position is threatened and contaminated—by playing with the devil, I become the devil. This kind of thinking surfaces especially in politics when not only is a politician of the opposing party rejected but everything he says is totally rejected, even if it means contradicting one's own position. How weak and confused is our identity, how shallow our understanding of personal freedom.

There is a way to have it all, a way to be the Self, to be the oher, to play with the devil, and to experience the unity of all sides. The conflicting desires for unity and separation can be satisfied by playing the game of Catch and Release.

Perhaps unity is valued above all else, but unity is sought by utilizing a brain that evolved to perceive differences and a sensory system that operates at a level where separation is obviously very real. However, self-actualization depends on managing disunity, opposition and conflict in a positive way.

Unlike the lower animals, which get trapped on one side of the fulcrum or the other, humans can maintain balance and avoid being trapped by consciously moving from one side to the other. Humankind has the gift of being able to occupy the golden fulcrum that balances polarities.

Life is a game or a stage play in which, as Shakespeare put it, "All the world's a stage, and all the men and women merely players." Success at the game of life comes from assuming a centered position that allows one to take the roles seriously but with a detached involvement and self-awareness that entails not only connecting with the other but, in a sense, actually becoming and then releasing the other to become the Self again. Remember, the other is anything outside of the authentic, subjective Self. The life-long paradoxical task is to become totally immersed in a dual role in which I go back and forth between being a subject and being an objective observer, or being a comedian and my own straight man. I call this the game of Catch and Release.

We call the game "Catch" even though the game obviously involves releasing the ball. I don't tell my son, "Let's go outside and play a game of release." Humans are naturally inclined to think of taking things in, holding on, maintaining control and possession as long as possible. We definitely have problems with the release part of the game.

Catch and release could be called on and off or life and death. The way to deal with the fear of death is to begin loosening attachments by playing the game of Catch and Release.

The cycle of constant releasing and attaching, giving and receiving is the universal dance of polarity as the one becomes the other, and the other comes back to the one. This cosmic relationship is profoundly illustrated by the bonding of man and woman in a single union essential to life in which the man releases sperm that is received by the woman. There would be no material existence if the atom didn't give up electrons to other atoms in ionic bonding, or share electrons with other atoms in covalent bonding. As I write this, I look out the window at our apple tree. By giving up its apples, by allowing the apples to fall, the tree provides apples that decompose into rich soil that not only allows the mother tree to flourish but also allows new trees to grow.

In so many countless ways, in the realms of the physical, biological, psychological and spiritual, we learn the lesson of reciprocity that giving is receiving. The problem for humankind lies in deciding how long to maintain possession. or how far to go in any one direction before stopping or returning. The game stops and the fun stops if the ball is kept too long. The game of Catch and Release is an on-going process that Cosmo plays with the universe, and humans are participating in a similar play within the play.

Although the other can never entirely become the one—I am not you—existence and human history suggest that oneness is the goal, and conflict may be the inevitable result.

Even though there are rules in life that insist on giving the other side a turn, and at least in sporting contests, the rules of the game and the referees set limits that allow both sides to take turns, once we have something in our grasp, we go to extremes to maintain possession. Possession, or attachment, is the catch phase, the life phase.

Politicians violate their own stated ethical convictions in order to hold on to their office at all costs, political partisans and religious fundamentalists reject compromise, unregulated capitalists tend to hold down wages while unions go on strike for ever higher benefits and wages regardless of the companies' ability to pay. It is hard for some of us to shut up and yield the floor once we begin telling our story. We see how Newton's First Law, the Law of Inertia, applies in the human world's attraction to extremes. Society works hard to establish and enforce rules and regulations that force us to release attachments to give the other guy a break.

Rules and regulations abound that reflect the attempt of society to allow both sides an opportunity to win, but in our minds we still tend to doggedly pursue our own selfish track in ways big and small. The human tendency is to push the rules to the limit. In football the line is narrow between offensive and defensive pass interference, corporations and nations act similarly by looking for every possible tax or regulatory loophole in order to keep on winning.

Our bodies don't make it easy to release attachments. The brain and nervous system are much more adept at forming attachments than at breaking them. Life is a constant tug-of-war between competing urges to become attached and to break attachments, to become involved and to escape involvement. The primary purpose of a life form, as far as the mechanism of evolution is concerned, is to perpetuate itself, which requires the organism to have a profound attachment to life and all that is required to sustain that life. We just tend to think that an awful lot of junk is necessary to sustain the good life, and we confuse attachments to Identifictions with life itself by maintaining an unyielding grip on beliefs, status symbols and traditions. We want the good times to roll on forever.

Progressing toward unity consciousness requires the conscious experience of the other which can only be obtained by releasing the fear that detaching from Identifictions will result in losing identity. The idea of Catch and Release is to find the other, understand it, release it and then return to the center where positions can be viewed objectively.

Sporting events are an intriguing metaphor for life because they incorporate all the elements we wrestle with in the larger game of life; conflict and competition, striving for goals, good versus evil, the struggle for survival, winning and losing and dealing with death. Winning in athletic competition requires many of the same skills and attitudes that are required to be a winner in life, including knowing how to play Catch and Release. Releasing possession allows each side a chance to score, and by insisting that teams and players change sides, each side must deal equally with the reality of losing or winning. In addition to simply ensuring order, rules and regulations allow teams the opportunity to experience reality from the other's perspective, to experience different wind, field and light conditions.

Every aspect of life entails a relationship between Self and some kind of other, between subject and object. Unlike a football game, few aspects of life are regulated in such a way that a change in direction is required. There is no referee to enforce time limits when you are feasting on that Thanksgiving dinner, telling stories to who you think is a captive audience, or pulling the lever on a slot machine. Catch and Release is God's dance of the moment. Maintaining balance in this dance of Self and other requires constant coordination of movement in a cycle between separation and unity, merging and distancing, knowing when to let go and when to reconnect.

The game of Catch and Release requires the recognition that each side is a winner in the big picture but also shares the experience of winning and losing in the moment. If the players in the game are really on the same side, then the terms "winning" and "losing" become meaningless. I am myself and I am you, I am the devil and the divine in an on-going cyclical game in which all participants share the same relationship with the Great Cosmo. The separate parts of existence are all interrelated to create the same team, just as all the cells and organs in the human body, and the stars, planets, dark matter and energy in the heavenly body are distinct yet interdependent.

We are participants in this game of life, but we are also objective observers. I attempt to see things from your point of view while still accepting the distinction of my perspective, but I understand that neither position is absolute or permanent. To some degree my very presence, even as just an observer, has modified your position. In physics, this is called the "observer effect," in which a photon utilized in observation alters the path of an electron. Your mere presence, and the presence of what you represent, alters my position. The authentic response is a return to the center.

Humankind plays with the Polarity Paradox the same way Cosmo does. Just as Cosmo's game is an eternal, universal spinning wheel balancing creation and destruction, separation and unity, uniformity and diversity, attachment and release, so we can partake in a similar never-ending cycle of Catch and Release between Self and other. But for God's sake, or Self's sake, remember to let go once in a while. Playing Catch and Release enables one to connect with the other while remaining rooted in the Self. Matter is ephemeral; it degrades and erodes, whereas the cycles and harmonies found in the universal process of connecting and disconnecting are eternal.

Looking out my back window as I write this, I am captivated by the contrasting silhouettes created by the last rays of the setting sun shining behind the bare twigs of an apple tree. At the moment there is nothing in my world more glorious than this sight. To catch this wonder, I had to momentarily release my attachment to writing and devote pure attention to the moment. I play Catch and Release with the moment as I dwell in delightful memories of the past or imagine future fantasies and dreams—yet this delight depends on understanding that rapture is ephemeral and slips away if the mundane and ordinary don't serve as contrast. However, the extended concentration necessary to finish this book requires momentarily losing balance in other areas, and this is the quandary, when to catch and when to release.

By playing Catch and Release we come close to resolving the great human dilemma created by the Polarity Paradox of wanting to protect the sanctity of separate individuality while also wanting the security of belonging to the group.

Catch and Release, or detached involvement, sees the truth from the perspective gained from momentarily pausing in the center during the journey from Self to other. It makes no difference whether the player is a comedian, politician, businessperson, athlete, or spiritual seeker. The comedian guides the audience, the politician knows the needs of the body politic, the businessperson understands the consumer, the spiritual leader empathizes with the flock, but truth is only gained by releasing attachment and returning to the center.

The centered perspective is home base for the enlightened Self. However, keep in mind that the center, like existence itself, is dynamic and changing. Thinking in terms of life being a process rather than a position, helps to avoid falling into the trap of categorization and stereotyping.

Life experience reflects the experience of the universe. My identity is now with the universe as I reject the feeling that I am all that matters. I experience unity consciousness, the unity of universal love rather than the separation of personal love. By resisting the shadows of the past, by allowing each moment to die, birth is given to a constant stream of new creations as the death of one thing gives rise to the life of something else. Ego death is as close as we get to the divine experience of the endless cycle of the duality of the yin-yang that is responsible for all that exists. Identity becomes universal as the movement between extremes in the game of Catch and Release becomes so fast that it appears there is no motion, just as the yin-yang are indistinguishable as the wheel spins faster.

We can either fight to stay on one side by playing our silly game of keep-away, or we can cooperate and share the ball in the game of Catch and Release.

Evolution Requires Motion

To be, to exist, is to flow and to move. Motion is an inherent property of matter, and of existence itself. The universe is intrinsically dynamic, so a universe without motion is cold and dead. Just as what appeared to be nothing exploded to form the universe, so Self must break out to connect with other. A greater Self is found by releasing false attachments to catch the perspective of other. The dance of the divine, the game of Catch and Release, like all cycles, requires motion. Unity involves Self moving toward other because without movement, there can be no progress; without movement there is no being.

Misunderstandings relating to motion are barriers to accepting the authenticity and value of Self. The classical Greek view, based on how reality is perceived by our limited senses, is that all motion is caused by external forces which leads to the common belief that a prime mover God must also be external to creation. However, modern science understands that motion does not come from outside matter but is intrinsic to and is a property of matter. This means that the creative motivating forces of the cosmos are intrinsic to the "things" of the cosmos. There are not two independent worlds, one of matter and one of spirit or energy; space-time-motion-gravity-matter-energy are all interrelated and can't be separated. In reality, since there are not really "things" as we think of them, the motivating force is all there is. Of course, this means that God, if there is a God, is not "out there" but is intrinsically linked to all there is—but of course I could be wrong.

Life has much to do with experience, and humans may be the way the cosmos becomes conscious of its own experience, and experience is related to motion. However, the wise and enlightened soul is not the person who has read the most books, accumulated the most degrees, or traveled the most extensively. It is not the experience itself that holds the key, but what is being learned from experience, and from the value placed on the experience. The "higher place" we are looking for is where we already are, and wisdom is gained from having the right attitude toward the moving moment.

It is pretty obvious that Catch and Release requires movement, since something has to change and move if nothing is to become something or for me to understand you. Cosmo is in a constant state of flux, and humans, being of the universe, are in a state of flux as well—as mentioned before, we are really human becomings rather than human beings. The constant speed of stellar molecules and the tug-of-war between expansion and contraction that governs the creation and destruction of stars, galaxies and the formation of elements and compounds seems to operate in our lives as the competing drives for the freedom of separation and for the security found in unity. The experience of both the universe and the human is to seek a dynamic balance or tension between opposing forces possibly by seeking a centered truce or homeostatic centered state.

Perhaps the grand desire of humans for unifying the one and the many, the Will to Unify, may be a manifestation of a universal evolution toward singularity. But unfortunately, although Cosmo and humans seek this balanced homeostatic state, the completely tension-free state is not only illusive but is also boring. Cosmo has to move, and the movement is toward finding out what the other has to offer. Without personal movement, which may entail conflicts and collisions, human and conscious evolution comes to a standstill.

To experience the other, which is the only way to Truth, one has to break attachments, to leave behind the tranquility of the Garden, and the process of releasing attachments can lead to tension, anxiety and fear. In the process of disrupting one unity, releasing attachments creates another unity at a grander level.

Motion is important physically, mentally, and spiritually. Without movement, the body's muscles, joints, and bones begin to age and deteriorate before their time, and without mental motion, the mind deteriorates. Just as motion keeps the material universe separated as well as together, motion keeps us apart from one another at the same time it brings us together.

Although physical movement is important, the essence of being human is the ability to transcend time and place by consciously, rather than physically, changing perspective, and allowing us to consciously move into the place of the other.

Physical movement is required for the health of the material body, and conscious movement is required for the health of the mind. The evolution of consciousness requires movement from Self to other in the attempt to reconcile polarity, but this conscious movement away from the ego-self involves detaching from the temporal world from which springs ego-identification. When someone asks us who we are, we think of what we have done, what we plan to do, where we are, and what we have.

Being in the Place of the Other

Meaningful connections can potentially be formed with any person, regardless of their race, religion, or background.

To be in the place of the other, it is necessary to release conscious attachments to Identifictions and to catch the truth from the other's perspective. Since time and place are unimportant and connections are not permanent, one need not feel threatened by the possibility of losing or changing one's ethical, sexual, religious, or political position by becoming the other. To accept your value and to understand your place, I don't have to become you physically or mentally; providence can be previewed in the mind. Being in the place of the other is finding the common ground, understanding the equivalence of Selves, and viewing the mountain peak from the other's perspective.

The fear that connecting with the other will result in losing connection with the Self is not a problem if your place is the same as mine, or if we can leave and then come back. Since identity is not a thing, time, place, or idea, there is nothing to lose and everything to gain by opening up to share the place of the other. In fact, if your place is the same as mine, if your truth is my truth, I don't have to go anywhere to find the truth of who you are. Fear of the other and fear of the loss of identity are overcome with the discovery that all Selves are equally vital parts of the interrelated whole.

The other day I had a conversation with an elderly lady in a senior living facility. This inconsolable woman poured out her grief over having lost her husband and son. She claimed that life was no longer worth living since the objects of her previous attachment had all vanished. As tragic as life can be, if we have faith that all of humankind possesses the same inner divinity, the potential always exists for forming profound new connections.

The release of Identifictions allows for the emergence of the greater Self to form the Super Connection that embraces you and all Selves. Be open to the truth of the other which is fundamentally your truth. Be careful of constructing impermeable boundaries. Avoid being trapped by attachments to false identities and limiting roles. If evil exists, attachment is at its root. Play Catch and Release; catch the devil, examine it, laugh at it, and then release it before negativity assumes an exaggerated reality.

My Truth Is Your Truth

> No man is an island,
> Entire of itself;
> Every man is a piece of the continent,
> A part of the main.
> If a clod be washed away by the sea,
> Europe is the less.
> As well as if a promontory were.
> As well as if a manor of thy friend's
> Or of thine own were:
> Any man's death diminishes me,
> Because I am involved in mankind,
> And therefore never send to know for whom the bell tolls;
> It tolls for thee.
> —John Donne

Humans are profoundly connected and similar in more ways than can be imagined; each of us shares a little bit of all others, one human being stands for all human beings. Wonderful things happen with the mutual acceptance of the Equality of Selves, for understanding the truth leads to knowing the connection of Self, God, and Other. And the realization of this trinity comes close to satisfying the human mission as well as satisfying the human's fundamental desire for the Super Connection.

The universal perspective sees humans as an integral part of a greater order in which separation and unity and all polarities are interdependent. I do believe that the great mission in the overall scheme is to seek resolution of the conflict between Self and other by realizing that neither side is permanently fixed, that each perspective leads to the understanding that your truth is also my truth.

The boundaries that separate Self from other are changeable; there is nothing absolute about the place twhere I am and the place where you are. The trick involves finding the right balance and knowing when to change position, knowing how far to go, knowing when to let the other in, and doing so without threatening the integrity of the Self. One of life's great fictions is that identity is threatened when barriers are lowered.

The feeling of belonging, the satisfaction of the desire for unity, comes from the recognition that the fears, desires, and dreams of the other are yours as well. With the recognition of this Equality of Selves, the souls of Self and other merge and expand as identities are shared. Separate but equal was ruled unconstitutional when applied to schools, bathrooms, and lunch counters, but in a cosmic sense we are separate yet equal. If you represent truth to the other, your identity will be included in the identity of the other. The truth of one becomes the truth of all. Many cells, many organs, but one body. The concept of Self expands to the universal scale with the recognition that Self confirmation and confirmation of the other are the same. Connecting with the Other expands the Self while separation restricts and isolates identity.

We are all formed by and respond to the same principles of existence in ways peculiar to our own unique perspective. You like country music, I like opera, but we both relate to the appreciation of the universal principles of rhythm, harmony, and the intervals of sound and silence that apply to all forms of music. Atheist and Christian alike share the fundamental desire to make sense out of the world and to find meaning in life. Understanding the homosexual experience may entail understanding the natural desire to unite with that which is similar to the self, and in the feeling of deep love that one man can have for another man, or one woman for another woman. The heterosexual experience may relate to the universal attraction between opposite poles, or to the desire to know and experience the polar opposite. Yet the striving for unity can be met within each of these experiences.

To fix a sagging economy a Republican may advocate reducing the number of regulations, lowering taxes, and encouraging the private sector to become more productive, while a Democrat may advocate regulating business, increasing taxes on the rich, and more government hiring. Underlying these policy positions is the shared commitment to improving the economy. No sane Republican is in favor of totally abolishing fees for services rendered, and no sane Democrat would advocate taking all the money from the rich. Often it is a matter of degree; how much to tax, how much to regulate. Absolute condemnation of the other is a sign of intellectual arrogance and lack of sophistication.

The hate, violence, and lack of compassion felt by even the most depraved criminal is sometimes part of our experience. To understand the murderer I recognize my desire to destroy that which threatens my physical or mental well-being, like when I am hounded by those inconsiderate tailgaters on the freeway. To one degree or another, harboring murderous thoughts is not uncommon; in 2005 a study on homicidal ideations among college students by J.D. Duntley found that 76% of women and 91% of men reported having at least one vivid, memorable homicidal thought. We cannot mentally ignore, destroy or totally reject the other in any form, not even so-called evil, for this will only lead to frustration, fragmentation and spiritual suicide. Once the negativity is recognized, deal with it and then let it go.

I do want to make it clear that by accepting non-being, the dark and demonic, and the opposing team, does not mean that life becomes less important or that the bad guys should be given free rein to wreak havoc and destruction. The opposition can't be granted an easy victory, and leaders at times need to take charge. Contrast and separation are necessary experiences; existence requires polarity. Of course, there are still choices to be made, there is a time for control and a time for release, there are enemies to fight and battles to be won.

Similarities are fundamental and inherent, theological, political or cultural variations are acquired differences that are simply unique expressions of fundamental similarities. We all want to love and be loved, the search for meaning and purpose is universal, all organisms fight for survival. To escape the drudgery or meaningless tasks of everyday life some people get drunk, others may engage in sports or escape by shopping or watching television, but all expressions are similarly motivated.

No matter what your position, whether pro- or anti-gun control, pro- or anti-capital punishment, atheist or theist, unless you are insane or totally delusional, there is a shared respect for life and for aligning the ways of society with the ways of natural order. Yes, hard choices must still be made and conflicts will still arise, but a conscious awareness and pursuit of discovering mutually shared universal truth eases tension, violence and animosity.

As civilization advances diverse perspectives are increasingly brought into closer contact. The survival of humanity depends on the mutual recognition and respect of our God-given similarities. Our earthly challenge and purpose is to actually understand Cosmo from each perspective, and to expose the fictions that cause separation. Respect for these similarities is respect for God and its creation.

Just as infinite universal experience must include "evil" and the finite, so at times the human experience includes being a "saint" as well as a "sinner." One difference perhaps between the saint and the sinner is that the saint is aware that personal power increases by sacrificing self-importance, which then allows for the connection between Self and other, whereas the sinner falsely believes that power and importance come from the Self standing supremely alone. The saint understands that while differences are important, fulfillment comes from unity, whereas the sinner suffers from the illusion that the only reality is the separate world of the ego or tribe.

Tremendous self-confidence is gained by accepting the Equality of Selves. As the truth and inherent value of Self is accepted, there is no longer the need for self-confirmation at the expense of others. With the understanding that the experience of the other is equal to the experience of Self, we have the confidence to reach out to others in the confirmation of their worth.

Solving the Mystery of the Ages

Prince Hamlet's famously opening soliloquy, "To be or not to be, that is the question," addresses the same fundamental philosophical and metaphysical question Martin Heidegger asks as he begins his *Introduction to Metaphysics*, "Why are there Beings rather than Nothing?" Logic tells us that it would make more sense for there to be nothing. The mystery of existence will always remain unsolved, however, the relevant question for humans is how do we respond to the condition of being? How we answer this question will determine the extent to which we find happiness and meaning.

The mystery involves finding the way to unity. According to many Christians, there is only one way, and that is through accepting Jesus as the Savior. All of us, whether religious or not, believe deep down in our hearts that our way is best. The truth actually seems to be that there are many paths to the mountain-top and the fun in life is enjoying the view from different perspectives.

When I look beyond the boundaries of physical appearance, social standing, Positions and Possessions, beyond religious and political beliefs, I begin to glimpse the subjective nature that we both hold in common. As the Identifictions of the ego-self slip away, I see much more.

Finding the way to the Super Connection with the Other that includes not just people but nature, situations, and existence, is accomplished by being in the humble center where Identifictions have been dropped. To the extent that we understand the greater connection, to that extent we begin solving for ourselves the mystery of Being.

The soul of the divine resides in Everyman. As I help you discover that truth for one is truth for all, as the two of us become one, I find that my identity, my sense of Self, has expanded perhaps in the same way that the raindrop gains by reuniting with the ocean. The ego's drive for power, popularity, positions, possessions—which is really the drive for unity being perverted—is only satisfied by understanding and sharing that truth for one is truth for all. We're all in the same boat, but the boat is ours, not mine, not yours, and the forces that form and rock and support the boat are the same for all of us.

Jean-Paul Sartre, though an atheist, said that God is man's

project, that is, man's quest for authentic identity is the search for God consciousness, for the I Am of absolute identity. If this is so, possibly man is God's project—or the project of the cosmos; God and man both need each other in the process of mutual self-discovery. Both God and humankind are not only hiding from each other but each is hiding from itself in a strange game of hide-and-seek, or catch and release, to find out what it's like to be the other, but the nature of God and human is similar.

If the infinite includes all experience, then, just as a coin must have two sides, it would seem logical that the universe must include, perhaps consciously, the experience of finiteness, or non-being. Just as the electron and proton share a necessary equality, so perhaps does the notion of a God that shares equally being and nonbeing. Humankind's role or purpose in this scheme may be to provide a timeless existence with the conscious experience of limitation and boundaries. The infinite Cosmo needs the finite human since the finite implies the infinite.

To continue the metaphor; God's game of hide and seek is momentarily over with the discovery that we share God's power of creation which leads to the discovery that we are actually God hiding from itself. In the process of centering and looking away from the imitation self of Identifictions, both God and man discover each other in the unveiling of the identity of the Universal Self. When I find God, it finds me. Both God and Man seek to know the other. This simultaneous discovery, this divine marriage of Self and Other, of subject and object, requires the temporary death of the empirical ego. The objective observer, the centered authentic Self, aware of the game, becomes closer to being the puppet master.

Humans may need God for the same reason that God needs humans, that is, if consciousness is a primary characteristic of both. When Identifictions are stripped away, consciousness in its purest form emerges as the centered authentic Self, or as Existentialists would call it, the transcendental ego. The necessary relationship between the transcendental ego and God (Other) is beautifully illustrated by Dr. Peter Koestenbaum's analogy. "If the transcendental ego's relation to the world is one of illumination, then otherness is needed to make the light visible in the first place. Light sent out to empty space illuminates nothing. Luminosity appears only when the light meets opposition and illuminates objects, even if the later are but particles of dust."

By rediscovering God's hiding place within—in this case, God being our creative power—the mystery of the ages is revealed, as is our mission and purpose. As we discover who we are by losing Identifictions, our mission—or God's mission—is realized as well. Perfect love will be attained as together God and human form the Super Connection that may resolve the mystery of how Self becomes other.

Releasing attachments to Identifictions finds one in the center zone. From the center you can look in all directions. Knowledge from the center begins to unravel the fundamental mystery of existence, the role of opposition, the Polarity Paradox of separation and unity, of Self and other.

Truth is found by looking outward and inward, catching and releasing, attaching and detaching, looking both ways, from up close and then from far away. To get the complete picture, to experience the truth at all levels, requires simultaneously occupying all positions of the spinning wheel of creation. We are here and there, I am you and you are me. Truth is a matter of perspective, and the greater the perspective, the greater the truth.

The more you discover the profound truth that opposites are complimentary aspects that comprise the unified whole you begin to see the connection and relationship of the parts to the whole, of the process and the product, of Self and other. The more I see and experience how the pieces of the puzzle connect, the more expansive becomes my identity. All connections are driven by the same fundamental desire to expand the Self. But understand that the puzzle is a never-ending process that is never complete.

Loneliness disappears and all fears are vanquished, including the fear of death, as the vast emptiness of the center is filled with the infinite other. Having given up ego defenses and attachments allows me to have the identity I have always sought. In the process of transcending the limited empirical ego-self, the

Authentic Universal Self is unveiled as the bond of connectedness is formed between you and me—the one now becomes the many and the many is incorporated in the one.

But remember, unity consciousness, the mystical union of Self and other, God and man, is not permanent. Absolute perfection, the state of enlightenment, is as elusive as is awareness of the present moment. The instant you are aware of the moment, it slips into the past, the moment you are aware of union, you lose it, just as the Big Bang occurred at the instant of the union of matter and energy.

The Gospel of Thomas quotes Jesus as saying, "If you bring forth what is within you, what you bring forth will save you. If you do not bring forth what is within you, what you do not bring forth will destroy you." What is within us? God is hiding out in us. "The mystery hidden for ages is Christ in you" (Col. 1:27). Jesus said in Luke 17:21, "Neither shall they say, Lo here! or lo there! for, behold, the kingdom of God is within you." Very simply, if we abide by the natural law and order of the cosmos, life is wonderful; if we don't, we are in trouble.

Questions of identity that split Self into subject and object, and fears of losing identity, are washed away by seeing my Self reflected in you. Having given up Identifictions I can now identify with you. The Equality of Selves sees the similarity and connection between Self and other and includes the understanding that problems and solutions don't appear in isolation, but the actions and attitudes you criticize in others are simply different manifestations of the truth common to all. Empathy and compassion grow with the recognition of our own capacity for hatred as well as love, for arrogance as well as humility. When we look beyond differences and bring others into our consciousness, they will respond with love as they find their personal worth validated. Identification with the other transforms negative feelings that arise out of the perception of separation, such as fear and egotism, into love and humility.

We have all met people with whom we have closely bonded, people who seemed to agree perfectly with our position, whether it be a shared connection with music, religion, politics or just sharing the same approach to everyday life. However, an authentic connection between two people goes deeper and beyond what we think. What is shared is more than just similar circumstances, interests, values or personality. What is shared in an authentically intimate relationship is the joy of recognizing and aligning with Truth. The joy in a shared aesthetic appreciation for Van Gogh's painting "Starry Night" is the recognition, usually subconsciously, of the painting's brilliant incorporation of the aspects of Truth that include balance, harmony, symmetry, contrast, polarity, motion, and resolution of polarity.

Understanding and applying fundamental life principles, powerfully expressed in Van Gogh's art, whether in work, sex, religion, sports, politics or any area of life, will enhance life connections. These cosmic principles can be a uniting force regardless of whether two people share the same religious or political views.

By destroying the wall of Identifictions that obscure Truth and separate Self from other, Cosmo's greatest mystery is revealed with the discovery that our shared purpose is to continually deepen the understanding that your truth is my truth and that we both share an equal relationship with the essence of the infinite. The imaginary power of separate beings is lost along with the fear of isolation, but what is gained is participation in the enlightened dance of unity, what is shared is the understanding that our common bond is with the infinite truth of Cosmo and the discovery that all my fighting to preserve my separation from you, all the trouble I have gone to in measuring differences, was for naught.

The intuitive Equality of Selves we all pursue lies trapped within each and every soul, struggling to be expressed. However, lacking universal perspective, this commonality is difficult to comprehend since much of it is beyond the capabilities of the physical senses and, unfortunately, it is our state of separation, our differences, that capture attention. Mere sensory observation gives an incomplete understanding of how we fit into the levels of organization, ranging from interpersonal relationships to the relationship with the cosmos.

One of life's frustrations is not being able to see what role we play in the broad scheme of this universal puzzle. Our problem may be like an isolated skin cell trying to comprehend its connection to not just other skin cells but trying to see its connection to the cells of other organs, or to the organism itself.

Fortunately, the gift of transcendence allows us to escape the exclusive view that confines Truth to one place as in a particular savior, which is often us, or to one religion or to one point of view, and to at least catch a glimpse of the unity that underlies diversity and separation. The miracle of transcendence allows us to detach from identification with the body and its problems, and to escape Identifictions.

Enlightenment approaches as we resolve the differences between Self and other by accepting the strange paradox that I am I but also that I am you, though from a different perspective. As the boundary between Self and other is crossed, we connect—I am you and you are me. Boundaries become places of connection rather than points of separation. With the release of Identifictions, self-interest becomes the same as interest in others, selfish needs become the needs of others. As the whole picture comes into focus, the devil is reconciled with the divine, and we begin to acknowledge the inner light as well as the shadow nature.

Detached from the illusion of a completely separate identity, the authentic Self overcomes barriers and breaks down boundaries that separate Self from other. Whether in the world of work or play, success requires being free of the limitations of false identities.

The Harmony of Opposites

Contrast is necessary for comprehending anything, since without something to contrast and compare, awareness has no object. One side needs the other, there is no creator without a creation, and there is no me without you. As Carl Jung said, "There is no consciousness without discrimination of opposites." In *The*

Supreme Identity, Alan Watts said, "Without evil to fight, good goes unrecognized, without ugliness to repel us, beauty loses its allure, and of course without death to abhor, there would be no life to love." Watts goes on to say, "From the eternal standpoint these oppositions are seen as harmony, the dark side ever enhancing the beauty of the light. Death renders life more lively; darkness makes light stand out more brilliantly; separation makes the union of love more intense." Watts explains that opposites go together transactionally, like buying and selling, for there is no sale without a purchase, and no purchase without a sale.

Humans reach for the divine while God seeks the profane. Humans seek God transcendence, God seeks human transcendence. In this way, God and humans complement each other; the existence of one requires the existence of the other, just as matter and energy and space-time are interdependent.

Humankind may have a special role to play in this dance of opposites, sort of like the neutron of the atom that says to its teammates, the proton and the electron, "Look you guys, I love you both. You may be polar opposites, but your electrical charges are exactly equal. Let's work this out." Occupying the fulcrum in the center of being creates the harmony essential to the natural sciences, literature, logic, mathematics, music, dance, love making—all forms of art and life. Existence is an equation in which one side requires the other side.

Nature establishes a certain symmetrical and rhythmical order to the way its laws of contrast are arranged, and it behooves humankind to coordinate life and thought with this rhythm. The universal law of contrast utilizes the principle of symmetry, balance, and equilibrium in the arrangement of contrasting elements such as intervals of sound and silence, relaxation-tension, expansion-contraction, matter-energy. These principles operate at every level, spiritual as well as physical, at every moment, in every realm.

No matter what the activity, success requires balancing opposites. Painters and photographers understand the interplay of light and dark and the elements of composition that include symmetry and balance of tones and shapes. A musician understands the symmetry involved in rhythm, the intervals of sound and silence, and the contrast of different pitches necessary to produce a melody with balance and symmetry. An athlete understands rhythm and balance as it applies to movement. Cooks balance flavors, such as sweet and sour, sweet and salty; conversation balances talking and listening; a wise politician sees the time and place for both the conservative and liberal approaches to governing in that there's a time to raise taxes and a time to lower taxes. There is a time for offense and a time for defense. The life-long challenge is trying to maintain balance, since the fulcrum constantly moves. Extreme attachment to any one side leads to a less satisfactory outcome.

Think for a moment how contrasting states fit into our lives. Pleasurable physical sensation often involves the contrast of contact and separation. Whether the activity is a massage, sexual intercourse, or the taste of foods, the alternating cycle of contact and separation enhances enjoyment, but only if the right balance is obtained between each cycle. Take massage for example. If pressure and squeeze alone are applied to the muscle without the release, the feeling is not pleasurable. Likewise for intercourse. Our most intimate encounter with the cycle of opposites, an act involving the rhythmical dance of Catch and Release, attachment and detachment, involves the most intense feeling of unity that a human can perhaps experience. The attraction that leads to this wonderful coupling is based on the universal desire to overcome the tension of separation by resolving contrasting differences.

The human brain, naturally geared to seeking equilibrium, finds symmetry, proportion, and balance aesthetically pleasing. A human figure is deemed attractive if it is fortunate enough to be endowed with symmetrical bodily proportions. The construction of any building must take balance into consideration. If trees aren't symmetrical, they lose balance and tip over. In physics, every action force is balanced with a reaction force, and mathematical equations must be balanced. There is the balance of nature, right and left hemispheres balance the brain, we seek to have a balanced personality, and of course we are advised to eat a balanced diet. The increasing number of people who identify as political and religious moderates see some truth to more than one position.

Yet, existence mandates extremes. Material existence depends on the extremes of the positive and negative electromagnetic charges in the atom that are exactly equal and opposite. There is a place for extremes when it becomes necessary to regain balance, and without disruption and imbalance there is no progress.

There is much misunderstanding relating to living a balanced life. We may think we must balance thirty minutes of reading with thirty minutes of physical exercise and an hour of work with an hour of pleasure. But think about it; can you think of a renowned artist, athlete, scholar, or entrepreneur who truly leads such a balanced life? It may be hard to imagine a Thomas Edison spending much time dancing or engaging in athletic diversions as a way to balance the time he devoted to his inventions.

Nothing moves without one charge being stronger than another. Perfect equilibrium is just another term for death, perfectly balanced forces lead only to stagnation. Not only is extreme action necessary at times to restore harmony and equilibrium but in keeping with Isaac Newton's first law of motion, unbalanced forces are required for movement to take place. Someone or some group often must break out, take charge, and herein humankind is confronted with the dilemma of how to disrupt the status quo and yet not be so disruptive that balance can not be restored. The existence of anything requires a measure of inequality. The moment of universal creation, the Big Bang, couldn't have occurred without an inequality of forces.

In a way, at least the perception of extremes is necessary to provide contrast. We lose balance as our lives lose contrast, but contrast is a matter of perspective. There's an old guy down the street who can afford to travel anywhere in the world but seems perfectly content to stay home, puttering in the garage, fixing broken electronic gadgets, and spending a few bucks at garage and estate sales. This guy adds contrast to his life with walks in the nearby hills and occasional forays to the nearby town of Gilroy in pursuit of some new broken gadget to work on. When I asked him to describe his dream vacation, he said he might like to visit Rabbit Hole, a small town in Nevada where, as a kid, he did some gold mining with his dad. Contrast is a matter of degree. Experience and the contrast of yin and yang can be minimal. To balance the bitter with the sweet, I enjoy a taste of chocolate with my coffee, but just a taste. I savor the rich creamy chocolate and let it linger in my mouth between sips of coffee. A small box of six pieces of gourmet chocolate can last me for weeks; being mindfully aware of the experience is what counts.

The never-ending Sisyphean challenge is seeking resolution of opposites while realizing that transcending separation or complete conflict resolution is unattainable—so although your truth is my truth, I am still I and you are still you.

Sex and the Will To Unify

The game of Catch and Release is most profoundly experienced during the act of sexual intercourse.

The existence of maleness and femaleness is one expression of the fundamental polarity of all reality according to Rollo May in his classic *Love and Will*. Sexual intercourse can be viewed as a metaphor for the resolution of polarity as the human counterpart of a cosmic process involving the interplay of positive and negative forces and the associated forces of attraction and repulsion. The Hindus see sexual intercourse as symbolic of the cosmic union of the female principle, the yin, and the male principle, the yang.

Catch and Release is expressed in the rhythmic dance of polarity as two partners engage in making love. Incredible tension builds up during sexual activity, and the climax is an equally wonderful relief of tension and a momentary entry into ecstatic chaos.

While a certain amount of stress and tension are necessary for health, tension by itself isn't particularly pleasurable. But it is the constant tension of modern life without any letup, the catch phase, if you will, without the complimentary release that creates the problem. Sexual intercourse, like so many activities, has a goal. When the goal is attained, tension is released. Life and existence require the rhythm of attachment and detachment, catch and release. If the partners lose the rhythm by remaining in contact too long or are separated too long, the excitement and pleasure are lost.

The desire for sexual intimacy, especially in the context of a loving relationship, is such a strong driving force because it offers the opportunity for humankind to satisfy the life-long search to resolve duality by uniting both the physical and nonphysical, Self and other, masculine and feminine in a way that doesn't threaten personal identity. Rather than sensory pleasure, what underlies the sexual drive may be the human need for intimate, self-affirming relationship. The sexual experience provides the most intense, ecstatic and satisfying experience available to humankind as lovers briefly participate in the cosmic act of creation that arose from the singularity that gave birth to the material universe.

Marriage is a cherished institution in part because it is the only way society sanctions as a means of satisfying the powerful urge for a profound physical as well as spiritual connection with the other. The temporary nature of the sexual act allows both partners to return to the secure state of separate identity, but lasting, deeply committed love relationships are challenging due to the feeling that if you get too close to your partner, if you love him or her too much, you lose who you are—you lose the freedom of separation.

Humankind evolved to function in a world of duality, and for this reason, I believe, we don't quite know how to deal with sexual union, or what scripture appropriately refers to as "knowing." As the act of primary human importance, we attribute both extremely positive and extremely negative attitudes to sexual intercourse. The intensely pleasurable feelings and thoughts of unity are troubling simply because they are the subject of such extreme concerns and desires. Separation is easier to deal with than unity, but unity, although a threat to the myths of identity, provides the greater reward.

This fear of forming connections is perhaps demonstrated by the uncomfortable reactions elicited by the act of lovemaking, the most obvious symbol of unity. Most things deemed desirable, such as beautiful people and flashy cars, are put on public display and talked about openly, but not "the act," which is to be carried out in extreme privacy and avoided as a topic of polite conversation, and can even be considered pornographic. We feel much more comfortable watching football games and violent movies than we do talking about love and beauty.

Consider the way we treat the act that comes closest to satisfying ultimate desires, the single act that is responsible for life itself. Since the very survival of Homo sapiens depends on sexual intimacy, one might say that it is the most important and positive human action. What is fascinating is that the English slang for sexual intercourse is at the same time perhaps the most useful and most prohibited word in the English language. The word "fuck" is used to describe the entire spectrum of human experience. When a person is rejected absolutely, they are told to "fuck off" or to "go fuck themselves." If a person is in a hopeless situation, he may say, "I'm fucked." But on the other hand, "fuck" is also used to emphasize the positive, as in, "That sunset was fucking beautiful."

Perhaps the controversy and confusion surrounding sexual intercourse is due to the paradoxical nature of the act. On one hand, intercourse is the ultimate expression of love, of giving as well as receiving. Yet the physical pleasure is extremely selfish, hence the act can provide a measure of satisfaction if carried out between two complete strangers, and the act can be violent, especially on the part of the male who, by nature, is the aggressor.

The eternal conflict of separation and unity is played out in the act of intercourse. Applying a few principles underlying successful living temporarily resolves the conflict during love making. The depth of the experience of love making is enhanced by realizing the importance of giving pleasure to the other person, releasing in order to receive. Just as in other human interactions, but especially apparent in love making, giving pleasure increases one's own pleasure.

True Love

One of the most beautiful experiences life offers can be found in the mature love between two people who drop protective ego barriers to form a union of the spiritual and physical. A couple may come from very different backgrounds, have very different approaches to life, and have no idea what is responsible for their mutually shared attraction other than the feeling that each of them completely and totally accepts the other. The paradox of their dual natures has been solved with the mutual acceptance of shared authenticity. Each person feels like he or she has united as one while still being totally accepted for his or her separateness.

Love derives its power from meeting the fundamental need of humankind for unity. The desire to love and to be loved is really the desire for oneness and for the unity of extremes. According to Paul, "God is Love (the ultimate connection)," and "if we love (connect with, understand) one another, God abides in us" (1 John 4:8, 12). To love is to accept that truth of other is truth of Self. You will love to the extent that you see the other reflected in you. Love resolves the Polarity Paradox by bridging the gap between Self and other.

Unfortunately, the instinctive longing for oneness often results in an abnormal attachment to the loved one and to the tendency to grab hold tightly, to want to possess the love object. We are so starved for the Super Connection with Self and other that once it is experienced, we don't want to let go. True love is the opposite of attachment. Attachment results in fixation on one pole to the exclusion of the other. The act of possession disrespects the free and independent nature of the beloved. When we seek to possess things, whether material things or friends or loved ones, the separate identity of these things is lost. Married couples lose the freedom of their separate and individual natures when they identify too closely with each other.

The game of Catch and Release entails the understanding that loving requires respecting each other's individuality. The lover doesn't force the love object to be or to act in a way that is contrary to its nature. A lover of a fine automobile knows just how far to push the engine, and uses the appropriate fuel and lubricants to keep the parts running smoothly. Loving my wife means allowing her to freely express her individuality and allowing her the time and space to pursue her own interests. Whether you are a woodworker, the President, a dock worker, or a spouse, respect must be shown for the free and unique nature of the object of your work or interest. And the relationship of course works both ways—the employee or student must understand the nature of the employer or teacher. When this relationship is out of balance, the wood warps, nations fall, workers strike, and marriages fall apart.

Respecting the unique nature of the loved one makes the beloved feel safe, knowing that independence is respected. The detached nature of love allows the natural cycle of separation and unity to operate in the game of Catch and Release.

There are two main stages in relationships. First there is contact and attachment. Two people establish either physical or mental contact during the initial period of the relationship. The second stage involves a period of letting go as each partner grants independence to the other. However, true love entails understanding that the Polarity Paradox of separation and unity can never be completely resolved. Although a primary desire in life is to overcome separation and at the same time maintain separate identity, true love understands that this can never be completely accomplished.

Love requires releasing control and attachment. In order to reach out to the other, one must empty attachments, including attachment to Self. If your arms are embracing you, you can't embrace the other. If you are filled with yourself, there is no room for other. As Mother Teresa said, "Even God can't fill what is already full."

All teachers at one time or another are asked by their students, "Why do I need to know this? I'm never going to use this knowledge." Paracelsus, the famous Renaissance physician said, "He who knows nothing, loves nothing." The more knowledge we have, the more likely we are to love. The more you know about something, the more you know what is required for it to flourish.

Love and unity consciousness is also fostered by seeing Self in other, by clearly seeing and emphasizing how you and I share fundamental truths. Meaning and purpose is realized as I experience that your existence is equal to mine. Total acceptance of other results in total acceptance of Self. For me to love you, I must love my Self.

Love and understanding are thwarted by not balancing perspective, by not stepping out of the empirical ego to view the world of the other from a psychological distance. Barriers to love are overcome by constantly changing perspective of looking up close and then far away. Many physical differences are noticed when two people are observed up close; viewed from afar, the differences are negligible. From a distance, a person's actions may appear to be thoughtless, like a driver who fails to signal while dangerously weaving in and out of traffic. I know such people, and an up-close and personal view often reveals a kind and generous nature. Unhappiness and dissatisfaction are caused by being trapped in this paradoxical world of separation and unity, which catches us simultaneously in a state of dualism and oneness. The material body and Identifictions cause up-close, uptight attachments while the mind transcends, loses attachments, and gains perspective from afar to view the big picture.

The good news is that perspective is easy to change. The most important step to accepting the Self is to see the value of where and who we are in the present moment. This only requires exercising the power of creation and knowing how to play Catch and Release.

Doomed to Choose

Humankind is doomed to be free and hence, doomed to choose.

Floundering about without the security provided by the boundaries of instinct or tradition, not knowing where to find happiness or the feeling of belonging, humans become filled with the anxiety of free choice. We find ourselves confronted with infinite choices about where the right position is and what possessions should be acquired to optimize survival. The more "civilized" we are, the greater the separation, the more choices we have and the harsher the judgments. High blood pressure, frustration, feelings of isolation and depression are the unhappy results of the anxiety of choice. The responsibility of knowing that our choices have consequences bears down on us.

We may envy the clearly defined roles of tribal cultures and caste systems, religious groups and political party members in which the members have the comfort of not only knowing and accepting their exact place but feeling that they are part of a unified whole. Elaborate rituals, traditions, castes, superstitions, and taboos bind members into smoothly functioning units that are accepted without question. Security and freedom from the anxiety of choice can be found by any group-think that leads the blind and willing.

The conscious power of choice—though choice is not as free as we think—confronts us once again with the fundamental aspect of existence addressed by Hamlet, "To be or not to be." Exercising choice is a sort of symbolic murder of alternatives. Whenever one choice is made, an alternative is killed off. Choosing one thing always involves rejecting something else. The choice of life and death, of being and nonbeing, to be an individual or to go along with the crowd is encountered every moment of every day. When I choose to go the way of the separate Self, I am rejecting unity that includes the other.

The simple act of choosing so dominates everyday life that its cumulative effect, though often unnoticed, is profound. The ever-present dilemma, so often referred to in this book, is deciding at any particular moment which side is best for the individual, society, nation, or planet, and when to separate and when to unite, when to catch and when to release. Physical, mental, and spiritual well-being depend on how Hamlet's question is managed in daily life.

Walking in the Wilds

Almost every day a neighbor and I take a long walk into the wilds of a hillside park. The following are a few critical judgments I made before our trek. I was barely out the door before noticing that some inconsiderate person's dog conducted its business on my lawn, a thoughtless neighbor had parked his car in front of my mailbox, and someone tossed litter in the street. The judgments and criticisms continued as I came to the beginning of the trail: graffiti on the park's restroom walls caught my attention, someone's dog was off leash. Each critical judgment had the effect of breaking connections.

The human tendency is to identify with the side chosen while rejecting the value of the side not chosen. We may not be aware of this, but it is there. And these little subtle and not-so-subtle judgments have a cumulative negative effect on the mind and body. Let's say I stop to pick up a scrap of litter on the trail. I would not have picked it up if I did not think littering was wrong. The thought flashes through my mind that I am glad I am not a careless and thoughtless person. I may even feel a little superior, because I am that rare good citizen doing an unsolicited good deed. I have no idea who dropped the trash, but at least I am superior to whomever it was, and since most of my walking partners never pick up anything, I am superior to them, as well (though they may be secretly judging me for picking up germs along with the litter and for putting the trail clean-up crew out of business). The Super Me lurks in the shadows.

But soon I found relief from judgements as I became absorbed in nature's perfection. A storm was breaking, and rainbows appeared in the mist as the sun streaked through the steel-gray clouds. I wondered at the special golden quality of the early evening light. I paid attention to the grazing cattle, watched the red-tailed hawks soaring overhead, and breathed in the delight-fully sweet vanilla-like aroma of the buckeye blossoms along the trail. Judgments and criticisms vanished, attachments to Positions and Possessions forgotten. How wonderful to be free of criticism and comparisons. The way the trees and grass grow, the pungent fragrance of sage, the warmth of the sun's last rays are totally accepted as perfect creations that are part of a perfect order in a perfect moment in which everything is a winner.

I believe the desire for authenticity is one reason the un-touched wilderness holds such an attraction. The natural beauty of mountains, trees, and rivers serves as testimony to nature's perfection and bolsters our faith in the natural order in stark contrast to the contrived, manipulated and unpredictable man-made civilized world.

We don't berate one tree for growing asymmetrically and praise another for growing straight, yet we find fault with peo-ple who are overweight and praise those who are slim. Believing that one part of a continuum must win out over other parts finds us in a world of duality looking for end points, for winners on one end and losers at the other, and taking notice of insiders and outsiders. It would seem ridiculous to say that respiration is more important than photosynthesis, or that the electron is more important than the proton, or that the crest of the wave has more value than the trough. Trying to find the way to enlightenment, or even the scientific endeavors to understand the fundamental nature of matter and energy, may be a futile pursuit when undertaken from a dualistic point of view.

The state of nature is one of the few areas of life that receives unqualified acceptance for being perfect just as it is. We natu-rally accept that trees don't have control over how they grow, neither is the stream criticized for eroding its banks, nor does the desire arise to rake up the fallen leaves in a forest or to pull weeds out of a meadow. I don't recoil in shock at the violence perpetrated by the strong against the weak when I spot a coyote pouncing on a mouse, and neither do I place blame on the mouse for its neglect of personal safety. The unified web of nature is accepted without judgement as being shaped by immutable and perfect natural forces in the same way that in the equation 2+3=5 we don't attribute less importance to the left side of the equation than to the right. Although these same natural forces help to shape human nature, often in subtle and imperceptible ways, the world of human actions comes under intense criticism.

Studies have found that walking in the wilds benefits concentration, improves memory, lowers blood pressure and heart rate, enhances the immune system, and speeds healing. Patients in hospitals who can see trees through their windows recover faster, a study by Dr. Patricia H. Hasbach showed that violent behavior was reduced when convicts at an Oregon prison watched nature videos. Walks in the wild replace the stress and tension of judging and evaluating with feelings of presence and unity. The challenge is to find the same beauty and awesome wonder in the human world of freeways and skyscrapers.

Don't the same laws of nature apply to the ways of people as to the ways of mountains and valleys? Aren't the amazing technological creations of the human mind just as awe inspiring as the Grand Canyon? Just as we are awestruck when gazing at towering redwoods so we can find awe and wonder in the brilliance of an Einstein for unraveling the mysteries of creation.

Communing with nature provides many health benefits, though researchers as yet don't know exactly why. Perhaps there are certain beneficial chemicals given off by the trees, or it may be that tension and stress disappear when critical judgments are left behind, or a psychological reset clears the mind of the clutter of civilization as we reconnect with our source. I'm sure that many factors are involved.

Having recognized the health benefits of being in nature, the Japanese government has established forty-eight official forest therapy trails for what they call "forest bathing," or shinrin-yoku. A Japanese study published in 2010 showed that walking through a forest for a few hours has measurable health benefits. Compared to walking in urban environments, studies found that people walking in a wooded area, or even just gazing at forest scenery for twenty minutes, had lower blood pressure, a reduced pulse rate, and a lower concentration of cortisol, a stress-related hormone, while increasing the production of disease and cancer-fighting white blood cells. Recent studies by Paul and Ruth Ann Atchley of the University of Kansas and David Strayer of the University of Utah found that spending a few days in the wilderness actually improved scores in creativity by 50 percent.

Over a hundred years ago John Muir recognized the value of connecting with nature. In *Our National Parks*, Muir said that "Thousands of tired, nerve-shaken, over-civilized people are beginning to find out that going to the mountains is going home; that wilderness is a necessity." The problem is that engagement in conversation with our hiking partner, or being plugged into electronic devices may decrease the health benefits offered by the sights, sounds and smells found in the wilds.

But it may not be anything about the natural world per se that's so good for us. The benefit may be that walking in the wilds fosters a state of unqualified acceptance of the here and now that temporarily suspends judgements and restrictive Identifictions. Accepting nature just as it is provides a refreshing relief from the critical judgments of the everyday civilized world that separate Self from other. The lowering of defensive barriers, and the momentary suspension of critical analysis allows for the expression of self-transcendent emotions such as awe, gratitude, admiration, compassion and elevation that foster the feeling of being connected to a greater reality. Research is beginning to show the many benefits to mind and body of looking toward a reality greater than the self.

These positive self-transcendent emotions emerge from a state of being open to the other, whether the other takes the form of people, nature, ideas, or existence itself. In contrast to the emotions of openness are the materialistic concerns that shut the other out; envy, covetous, resentment, anger and jealousy. The feeling of awe may arise with the awareness of being in the presence of something that transcends everyday experience, something vast, beyond comprehension in its beauty, grandeur or power; the unending dome of the night sky, a magnificent cathedral, a brilliant child prodigy's gymnastic prowess, or even the personal discovery of a life-changing philosophical insight.

Being awestruck by immensity and the eternal imbues one with feelings of insignificance with the recognition of our comparative insignificant size, power or influence. Knowing that the sense of awe contributes to the formation of religious beliefs, religious groups have constructed awe-inspiring mosques and cathedrals that enhance the feeling of connection to a greater power. Is it then possible that an enlightened understanding of one's intimate connection with the infinite might diminish the need for religion and dampen the sense of awe?

Being in a state of awe allows us to lose selfish concerns and refocus attention to humbly recognize participation in something greater than the individual. Judgements fall by the wayside as whatever occupies the present moment finds absolute acceptance. There is no limit to what that something in the moment may be, but that brief loss of the limited self results in the Super Connection with the expansive universal Self that unites subject and object, Self and other. This total absorption in the unified moment erases concern with polarities, ends and beginnings, good and bad. For a brief instant, reality is unified, the fractured puzzle is complete at last. This is Nirvana; no time, no differences, no death, just Oneness.

Needless to say, there are many health benefits to feeling awe, gratitude and the rest of the positive, self-transcendent emotions, all of which assist in the realizing of human potential for finding the Super Connection. A study conducted at the University of California at Berkeley, published in the April 2015 edition of the journal, Emotion, co-authored by Jennifer Stellar from the University of Toronto and Dacher Keltner from the University of California at Berkeley, found that regularly experiencing awe has anti-inflammatory benefits.

Losing selfish concerns, feeling connected to a larger world naturally encourages the expression of the self-transcendent emotions of empathy, compassion, elevation and joy.

Robert Emmons, a professor of psychology at the University of California at Davis, reports that gratitude research suggests that feelings of thankfulness have tremendous value in helping people cope with daily problems, especially stress, and to achieve a positive sense of Self. People who describe themselves as feeling grateful to others and grateful to either God or nature for the gift of life tend to have higher vitality and more optimism, suffer less stress, and experience fewer episodes of clinical depression than the population as a whole.

Inject the wow factor into your life! Be inspired and awestruck by the miracle and wonder of being itself. Allow yourself to exuberantly exclaim, "Life, you're wonderful! It's wonderful to be free in spirit! I'm wonderful. People are wonderful!" How good this makes you feel, how your spirits and mood are lifted, how exhilarating to exalt in thunderous applause for the gift of creation. Remember the marvelous mundane!

Sad that the rarity of this golden sentient moment is not only taken for granted but is actually complained about. The surprisingly high level of well-being among the disabled, the chronically ill, and the elderly is likely due to their realization that life, good health, and a good working mind are of short duration. However, we do not need to be ill or old to realize this, so why wait to reap the benefits.

Living the Link

Live the link. See yourself as an integral part of the community, family, neighborhood, nation, human race, planet, universe, and if you are so inclined, be conscious of your connection with the divine. All of these levels overlap and are interrelated, and you are a part of each one. When you pick up a small bit of litter, be aware of your participation in maintaining the appearance of the community.

Feeling, thinking, and living the connections at different levels of organization is a way to increase flow, which is one key to happiness, meaning and spirituality. Engage in activities for their own sake, be conscious of connections with the greater whole. As connections expand, so does the Self.

The individual's failure to see connections to the big picture has ramifications in every area of life. A president can't take office in a democracy without being voted in by the electorate, but many people don't vote because they believe their single vote won't make a difference. This same level of thinking leads to the belief that one little piece of litter or plastic won't despoil the earth, so why bother recycling or conserving the earth's resources. It may be true that individual acts often don't count for much, but my personal belief and experience is that a more profound life experience is attained by (generally, not always) following the advice of Immanuel Kant's categorical imperative, "Act in such a way that your actions should become universal law."

Don't just use words to mouth clichés, or robotically express safe opinions but occasionally live and experience the ideas being expressed. Don't just say, "What a beautiful sunset"; live, feel, and wonder at the radiance and glow. Live your words, feel your thoughts, feel your part relating to the whole.

The bond strengthens by appreciating one's contribution to each level. Marvel at the wonders of the night sky, luxuriate in the warming rays of the morning sun, feel your connection with the cosmos. Don't just go through the motions of voting, be grateful for the right to vote that links you with the national level.

Living the link is experienced as the centered authentic Self is freed from Identifictions and sees the principles of existence (polarities, symmetry, cycles) which build the scaffolding on which is formed our attachments, loves, joys and fears and all of our responses to the conditions of existence.

CHAPTER 7

THE SEARCH FOR AUTHENTICITY

"Man is never so authentically himself than when at play."
Friedrich Schiller

Let's Get Real

The hippies were like children; "flower children" they were called. Their uninhibited dancing, free expression, nonjudgmental attitudes, and costumed appearance were contagious and had quite a liberating effect on an over-controlled, uptight society. We love to be around children because of their refreshing spontaneity, unpretentious authenticity, and unqualified acceptance of others. Children provide grown-ups with the excuse to express the wonderfully spontaneous and purposeless child within, so long repressed and now covered up by layers of propriety and preconceived notions. Playing with children provides a socially acceptable way to escape the confines of the roles imposed by society.

Around children we can skip, sing, play hide-and-seek and act as foolish as we want and still be accepted. I can actually look at a child's face and smile without either one of us feeling self-conscious or telling the other, "Hey, weirdo, what are you looking at, and what's so funny?" Jesus knew what he was talking about when he said become as little children to enter the kingdom of heaven.

Unfortunately, the transforming social movement of the hippie peace-and-love era of free expression soon lost its balance in an atmosphere of uncontrolled chaos. The child, like the untamed id, is true to its nature, but like a wild animal, the child lacks the perspective to step out of itself to connect with the other, or to evaluate its own behavior. Because of the child's unrestrained and uninhibited nature, it must at times be restrained by the parent. The hippie movement lost the control and organization necessary to function as a regulated, ordered society in which people must follow rules, get up early, fight commute traffic, and labor from 9 to 5 in some cramped cubicle.

The hippies lost their natural spontaneity and became captive of just another structured societal norm; if you didn't have long hair, wear sandals, and spend your waking hours stoned, you weren't with it. Like children, hippies were free and spontaneous but lacked wisdom and perspective. Like most of us, the intellect and objective mind of the hippie was overruled by emotions and sensory experiences. Lacking a solid philosophical and psychological understanding of their insights, and falling victim to extremes, the movement crashed.

We hunger for authenticity in response not only to the numerous ways reality is manipulated, but in response to how we feel manipulated. The need for authenticity is driven by what we perceive as our own lack of genuineness and by the desire to find out who we really are, what we really want and desire. In so many ways we are fakes by accepting without question the rigid roles and beliefs thrust upon us by family and culture.

We want to escape a phony world to find Truth, the absolute, unadulterated, unfiltered truth, stripped of the layers of political correctness. We all share a passionate desire to be more intimately and profoundly involved in the experience of living. The spontaneous joy and exuberance of our uninhibited inner-child have been sucked out of life by mind-numbing routines, outdated conventions, and the pressure to conform. We want more out of life than what we are getting.

So accustomed are we to conforming to the expectations of others that we aren't even aware of our alienation. The authentic Self has been repressed for so long that its very existence is doubted. Attitudes and behavior are under such tight control that we don't know who we really are or what we really want. We become as boring and unimaginative as the grey and white cars we drive and the grey, white, and brown houses in which we live. The alienation is worse for some people, such as politicians and corporate strivers, who have had to conform and compromise in their climb up the ladder to success and power. To one degree or another, the compromises required to function in a civilized world eat away at authenticity.

Often without being aware of it, every person has a strong desire for what Abraham Maslow, the founder of humanistic psychology, called self-actualization. Self-actualization is the realization of one's social, intellectual and creative potential. However, according to Maslow, full human potential and authenticity can't be reached until certain basic needs are met that are ordered in a hierarchy ranging from the physiological survival needs for nourishment, sex and health, to love and belonging, and then to self-esteem and respect. Only after these basic needs are met does one begin to reach for self-actualization.

Modern technology makes it easier than ever to generate fakes. With Photoshop, face-lifts, Botox, computer graphics, virtual reality, synthetic materials, and digital as well as genetic manipulation, it is hard to tell what is real from what is fake. An analysis of Twitter posts by the Massachusetts Institute of Technology Media Lab between 2006 and 2017 found that fake news travels six times faster than real news.[1]

The more complex and highly developed the society, and the more basic needs are met, the stronger becomes the desire for meaning, authenticity and the realization of full human potential. Unfortunately, as civilization advances technologically, authenticity decreases. Since nature seeks balance, the

---

[1] Science, March 9, 2018, Vosoughi, Roy, Aral, "The spread of true and false news online"

consequence of any extreme is to tip the balance toward the opposite pole. As the cover-up increases, so does the desire for the genuine article.

The desire for authenticity is expressed in so many ways: the appeal of organic foods and natural fibers, the practice of holistic medicine, the anti-vaccine craze, the movement to preserve historic sites. The term "authentic" or "natural" appears on countless products as an advertising ploy. "The Straight Talk Express" was the slogan on the side of the bus that transported Republican presidential nominee Senator John McCain. Similarly, his opponent, Barack Obama, promised to be a different sort of politician, the kind we all want, one who can be trusted to tell it like it is. Donald Trump was elected President in part because his supporters perceived him to be outside of the corrupt, inauthentic political establishment.

Uptight and Out of Sight

Pressure to conform, to get along and avoid conflict determines every aspect of a person's life: the model and color of cars we choose, clothing styles, personal appearance, how we eat, what we eat, what we believe, what we say, and what we do. Every area of life is controlled by rules, conventions, and notions of proper behavior set by those who, in many cases, are even more screwed up than we are. To quote Ralph Waldo Emerson, "To be yourself in a world that is constantly trying to make you something else is the greatest accomplishment."

Acceptability falls within an absurdly narrow range. An almost imperceptible bit of chocolate stuck on the upper lip will drive people crazy, and a microscopic stain can relegate an otherwise brand-new sweater to the trash heap. Nothing is more embarrassing than clapping at the wrong time at a performance. A car that hesitates more than a few seconds when the traffic light turns green risks getting blasted by honking horns. And as previously mentioned, the many sanctioned topics of polite conversation frustrate attempts at establishing deeply meaningful connections.

Examples of how we are controlled and uptight are so prevalent that most of the time we are oblivious to our imprisonment. Just yesterday my wife and I went to a friend's buffet dinner. The buffet line was backing up and I was hungry, and when I'm hungry I am apt to lose control. Feeling sorry for the other hungry partygoers, but more so for myself, I stepped out of line. Enlisting the help of another guy who didn't mind embarrassing his wife, we pulled the table away from the wall and started a second line on the other side of the food display to speed things up. After dinner we drove downtown to a local coffee shop to hear a free blues concert. Now these guys were really rocking, but you'd never know it by looking at the audience. Oh, there were some of us who tapped our fingers a little, or swayed a little to and fro, but always under proper control. For the most part, we were all pretty uptight. People usually don't dance in coffee shops, and having embarrassed my wife enough for the night, I kept myself in line by staying in my seat.

Social ostracism or worse is risked by anyone deviating very far from these carefully constructed boundaries of behavior and belief. People are fired, blacklisted, transferred, imprisoned, tranquilized, and even killed for deviating from the norm—though not yet for the stain on the sweater. And yes, boundary breakers can go too far. There is always the tendency toward extremes. However, it is extremes that civilization seeks to control. Hermann Hesse's semi-autobiographical novel *Steppenwolf*, widely popular in the 1960s, eloquently describes the stultifying effects of civilization's attempt to control extremes:

> What we call bourgeois . . . is nothing else than the search for balance. It is the striving after a mean between the countless extremes and opposites that arise in human conduct. . . . It is open to a man to give himself up wholly to spiritual views, to seeking after God, to the ideal of saintliness. On the other hand, he can equally give himself up entirely to the life of instinct, to the lust of the flesh, and so direct all

> his efforts to the attainment of momentary pleasures.
> The one path leads to the saint, to the martyrdom of
> the spirit and surrender to God. The other path leads
> to the profligate, to the martyrdom of the flesh, the
> surrender to corruption. Now it is between the two,
> in the middle of the road, that the bourgeois seeks to
> walk. . . . In short, his aim is to make a home for
> himself between two extremes in a temperate zone
> without violent storms and tempests; and in this he
> succeeds though it be at the cost of that intensity of
> life and feeling which an extreme life affords.

We are all aware of these absurdities and at times would like
to shout, "The emperor is naked!" The instinctive desire for authenticity and free expression leads to rebellions against repression and controls. The hippie and counterculture movement, be-
ins, encounter groups, and cultural and political revolutions of
the late '60s were in reaction to the uptightness and rigidity of
the '50s. The desire arose for authentic encounters with the Self
as well as with others. Mind-altering drugs blew the minds of
kids who were raised by a controlled, uptight society that until
1965 still had racially segregated hotels, restaurants, and bathrooms in certain sections of the United States.

Don't Lose Control

The deep-seated human need for order is possibly a manifestation of the universe seeking order. However, as experienced
by humans, Cosmo's need for order also finds expression as the
need for power and control. The exaggerated drive for power
stems from the mistaken belief that the realization of human
potential depends on keeping you out by maintaining distinct
boundaries between Self and other — of course, just the opposite
is true, boundaries must be permeable.

You name it, someone wants to control it, box it in, and we all
want to break out, to be free. The desire for freedom is as strong
as the desire for power: parents and teachers control children;

scientists try to control the weather; we control our pets, weeds, finances, appetite, sexual urges, emotions, and language; and dictators try to control everything. In countless ways society, the government, and corporations want to control us; what we eat, what we read and watch, where we go, what we buy and sell, what we build, how we play and work, every aspect of life seems to be under someone's control.

In addition to being concerned with controlling the self or others, the civilized world attempts to gain control of space, time, and material. Faster and faster modes of transportation and satellite phones attack the limits of time and space, countless mechanical devices augment limited muscular strength, computing devices overcome limited intelligence, and so on. Human inventions and creations at times are attempts to make the finite infinite.

Sometimes we mistakenly feel that we can't get too excited about forming connections, because we want to be cool and detached and have the god-like power to be above it all, to be in complete control. Hollywood often portrays the mythic hero as calm, unemotional, unexpressive, slow-walking towers of controlled strength. "Don't get so carried away, control yourself, don't get so involved," are common expressions that indicate a reluctance to fully and enthusiastically connect.

American culture views control differently for males and females. It is more socially acceptable for females to have the freedom to sing, dance, laugh, and cry whereas males are expected to be under tighter control. During sexual intercourse, women expect men to maintain control in order to please the woman, who is urged to abandon herself in uncontrolled ecstasy. And possibly because men are under such tight control, they are the ones who suffer a greater incidence of mental illness.

One of the ways society maintains control and order that was discussed in the section, "What's Your Purpose?" is by sanctioning a time and place for self-expression. Holiday celebrations are acceptable outlets for the expression of joy and laughter and sporting events provide an excuse for expressing anger and hostility as well as wildly exuberant support of "our team." Singing can take place on stage or in a choir—if you are good enough, that is. If you can't carry a tune, you can still sing along with a group. We are conditioned to believe that there must always be outside sanction for the expression of ideas and behavior.

Why do we allow ourselves to become separated from experiencing life by the boundaries of symbols, convention, and conformity? Why the reluctance to enthusiastically express our feelings? We want to love, laugh, and dance, be silly, joyful, and enthusiastic, but always under proper control, being careful not to get too carried away, being careful not to create the wrong impression, always remembering that there is a proper time and place for everything. Too often, when things are pretty darn good, we still hold the applause. Numerous studies show that zest for living is a character trait that is highly correlated with happiness.[2]

The worldwide growth of the Pentecostal branch of Christianity may be due in part to their acceptance of spontaneous, uninhibited and enthusiastic expressions of joy and praise. Perhaps the same repressed need for intense experience partly explains the popularity of mass celebrations, festivals, sporting events, and protest marches and demonstrations. These activities provide an acceptable stage for the intense involvement of the flow that is missing from day-to-day living. It is really too bad that so many excuses are needed for expressing a passionate love of life.

The exaggerated need for control, power and approval is the consequence of attributing too much value to external authority rather than relying on the truth of the inner reality of the creative mind. As a result of the illusion that reality is only what can be detected by the physical senses, we are convinced that Truth occupies locations outside of the present Self in some different place from where we are now. Every area of our lives is affected: relating with people, singing and dancing, sexual rela-

---

[2]   Park, Peterson, and Seligman, 2004 *Strengths of Character and Well-Being*, Journal of Social and Clinical Psychology: vol. 23, no. 5, pp. 603–619

tionships, exploring new and innovative ways to deal with situations and problems, exploring new ideas that are contrary to accepted modes of thinking, and relating to the natural world and the authentic Self. Frustration, discontent and the stifling of self-expression and autonomy are due to the related Myths of the Missing Piece and the Perfect Place both of which falsely claim that because the Truth we're looking for depends on finding the perfect external conditions therefore affirmation and validation also depend on outside approval.

Thinking that identity, purpose, and happiness depend on things external to the Self shapes so much of our thinking and behavior; we are constantly stepping out of the present, away from I AM, in the search for goals and end products rather than enjoying the process. Don't let the false belief in external truth deny you the richness of experience. Accept the authority of your inner power of creation and see the truth of the perfect present. The ultimate connection depends on releasing the restrictions on the inner Self, so go ahead and sing and dance and laugh, even if there is no accompaniment, no stage and no audience. The more aspects of your being that are expressed, the more complete will be the life experience.

The reality of separateness seems greater than the reality of unity and oneness. My separation from you, and the boundaries that separate us are more obvious than our similarities for reasons previously discussed. And as materialists who lack confidence in the truth of the unseen inner authority, it is easy to succumb to the crowd as the source of confirmation and truth.

One of the reasons self-expression is stifled has to do with a lack of trust in human nature. The fear is that removing society's shackles would release some crazy, out-of-control monster-self to rape, pillage, and run amok. Order and control has to be maintained at all costs, so society imposes strict controls on self-expression. And when laws don't restrict self-expression, then social ostracism, peer pressure, and political correctness do the job. But keep in mind Cosmo's cyclical nature; order tends toward extremes, the consequence of which is a return to chaos.

Drop the Role, Be Weird

We play so many roles. Circumstances, of course, require participation in roles, but at times roles are adhered to so rigidly that authenticity and connections with Self and other are impeded as roles become tied up with self-identity.

I may begin the day as a parent, seeing that my young son is dressed appropriately, well-fed, hugged, and sent off to school with the encouraging words to be a good boy and to always do his best. I then assume the role of a commuter as I drive off to work, being sure to courteously follow the rules of the road. The roles of teacher, colleague, customer, and finally, husband will complete the day. Other abstract roles further complicate matters as I may identify with being a person who is always understanding, loving, rational, stable, rational, wise, intelligent and so forth.

It is so easy to get stuck in roles. By identifying with roles we become confined to certain ways of acting and thinking that block connections, stifle authenticity, and prevent unity consciousness. The other, as well as the Self, is limited by our conception of what is required for a particular role. Each role obviously has certain requirements; teachers and parents must serve as positive role models and must maintain a balance between being a friend and being a leader. But strict identification with roles limits identity and steals from the wonder of infinite being.

Roles interconnect and overlap, but problems arise when we become frozen in roles. We may condemn a person for something they said or did to offend us, and then we assume the role of the victim and give the other the role of offender. Even though their so-called offense is not who that person really is, we have cast them permanently in that negative role, just as kids cast parents in a permanent role and vice versa. Disagreements fracture relationships when identities are caught up in political or religious viewpoints that permanently brand a person as a Liberal or Conservative, believer or skeptic. The disagreement is then magnified, overgeneralized, and the area of disagreement spreads over the entire being of the other as we say something like, "Oh, that guy's a socialist, can't reason with him." Or we may cast a wider net over an entire group of people, but then, I have already discussed how stereotyping is a lazy way of ordering life and elevating self above other.

A good stage actor has the objectivity to become detached from the role being played. Paradoxically, the actor does take the role seriously, genuinely laughing, crying, or exhibiting whatever response the script calls for, while also being detached enough to understand that the role is simply an act to be played. This detached perspective is achieved by playing Catch and Release. The best actors can play drama as well as comedy.

Shakespeare said, "All the world's a stage." Being on the grandest stage of all, the stage of life, we are living the actor's dream as we find all possible roles open to be played. The Academy Award is forever ours on condition that the role be understood. Life is an interactive role in which the actor is simultaneously playing the audience and the audience is playing the actor. Like any stage actor, we must take the play seriously while still realizing that life's roles are games to be joyfully and lightly played out.

As you begin expressing your inner truth, be prepared to be labeled as being slightly weird or eccentric, because when you don't fit neatly into any particular slot, you will appear to others to be somewhat unpredictable. See this as a compliment that you have escaped the boring, inauthentic, self-possessed, unconfident existence that society considers normal. In fact, as you give others the love and attention they desire, and as they see you for the happy, natural person you are, they may become "weird" themselves as they desire what you have.

I always considered it a compliment when my junior high students would say, "Mr. Watts, you're so weird." Adolescence is often an awkward age because the youngster is just emerging from the spontaneous life of the child, who lives for no other purpose than to experience the process of the surrounding world. Entering a world that requires critical judgments, goal setting, and striving for high academic or other standards, the child begins to worry about just what is or isn't considered to be normal behavior. I would tell my students that often the people who are really weird are those rigidly controlled individuals who pretend to be seriously normal.

The trick is to change sides, to understand the truth of both sides and yet be able to return to the middle ground of objectivity. The fear is that place will be lost by attributing absolute value to the other, and if place is lost, then so is identity. We want to be in the place of the Other, but we also want the security of being able to return to the safety of our own unique identity. However, place can be released by playing Catch and Release.

Exchanging places with the other can be done consciously, outside of place and time. The truth of the authentic Self, being based on universal principles, is beyond the limitations of space-time. The real Self, once unveiled, can no more be threatened or lost than can the law of gravity.

One key to enlightenment is to avoid identifying with the identifictions of Positions and Possessions as they become the roles and props of life. Don't become so attached to the symbol that you confuse Positions or Possessions with the authentic Self, the subject of creation. Even though some aspects of a role may accurately reflect your talents and circumstances, the symbols are not you. They are mere representations of the pure experience we are seeking.

Conforming Nonconformists and Weirdos

In some way, we all think of ourselves as being unique individualists, outsiders who are a little weird. But weirdness is often thought of as a positive attribute since many so-called weaknesses may actually be strengths and a sign of true normality — society's norms are by no means the final word on defining normal behavior. Individuals who accept the fallacy that importance is related to separation seek approval by being included in one group but separate from another. To one degree or another, this is what humans do—we join the in-group out of a desire for unity while our desire for separation and uniqueness causes us to put down the out-group. For reasons that would be the topic of another book, the pull between the conflicting desires for separation and unity seem to be on the increase as witnessed by the increase in political partisanship and the cynical distrust of established political parties.

Alleged nonconformists can actually be the biggest conformists of all. Although we pretend not to care what others think and proudly declare independence of thought, we are still conformists seeking normality and acceptance. Pretenders to liberation, in the attempt to maintain the image of nonconformity, may be more rigidly controlled and conformist than the conformists they criticize. These misguided souls have actually restricted their freedom by rigidly conforming to some group's narrow definition of what to believe, how to dress, and how to act. The hippies of the '60s and '70s were especially proud of their freedom and individuality, yet no self-respecting hippie would be caught dead with shoes, short hair, or a clean-shaven face out of fear of not being accepted by the norms set by the "nonconforming" hippie subculture. By emphasizing superficial differences, nonconformists fail to connect with the source of authenticity and human commonality.

Breaking Free

Freedom is in the mind.

Freedom from uptight societal conventions can take place in the mind as a conscious realization, just as the experience of nothingness and ego death can take place in the mind. The realization that brings us back from the encounter with meaninglessness is that out of nothing we are free to attribute absolute meaning to whatever we choose. So even if we seem to be under tight external controls or physical limitations, in a wheel chair, locked in prison or under social constraints, the conscious mind is still free. It is the freedom in the mind that breaks through boundaries.

There is more to authenticity or to being a truly liberated nonconformist than just challenging society's prevailing assumptions by dressing in rags, wearing nose rings, growing shaggy hair, and dancing in the street. Being in contact with the Truth does lead to conformity, but to an authentic, reality-based conformity in which the Self conforms to natural order rather than to the order of society.

The German philosopher, Georg Hegel believed that the first stage in being human involves the process of habituation—when the patterns of culture are assumed—regarding everything from the style of dress to the proper way to hold a fork. As people mature, they may begin to question the accepted conventions of society and come to believe that being free requires throwing off all conventional attitudes and behavior. Dualistic, black-and-white thinking is then likely to give rise to a rigid rejection of all authority. After the Spanish Civil War, when the anarchists were briefly in control of Barcelona, even one-way streets were abolished as a symbol of the old authority. Hegel goes on to say that by reaching the third level of development, the free man begins to accept the practicality of acquired habits. Routine and ritual provide structure for life's experiences, just as the physical body provides a structure that protects the life process. The liberated authentic self-realizer is aware of the practical reasons for conformity.

A truly out-of-control liberated person—who is actually in control—realizes that inner freedom from control is what is important in forming connections. An authentically free person in harmony with Cosmo may actually appear to be highly controlled and conformist. Out of consideration for neighbors and those nearby, the free person will exhibit polite and unobtrusive manners in public, and his or her yard is likely to be at least reasonably well maintained and may actually be attractively landscaped combined with a house beautifully adorned with paintings and art objects. The principles of aesthetics are the principles of nature's order; being in harmony with Self is being in harmony with nature as other. We will likely find a house that is well organized and clean for practical considerations, since it is easier to locate things if a house is neat and orderly. The authentically liberated person may not stand out from the crowd in any noticeable way. Pretenders to enlightenment, who are stuck at Hegel's second stage of development—which questions and challenges convention—may brand this apparent uptight conformer to be a traitor to the cause of nonconformity, when in reality this person may be the freest of all. Freedom in the mind is what counts.

Conformity is helpful and practical at the beginning of many human endeavors, whether it be a way to tie shoes, swing a tennis racquet, write a novel, draw a picture, prepare a meal, or arrange a business deal. First the basic techniques of structure and form are learned. With the advanced understanding that comes from the centered position, preconceived notions and conventional habits can be released, allowing for the creation of new forms.

The self-realized person, is not a slave to tradition, routine, ritual, or ceremony. Innovations in all fields, whether art, business, science, or spirituality, require an initial knowledge and mastery of certain fundamentals; it is then that the innovator gains the confidence to break from traditional roles and practices. Picasso was a master of the representational, realistic style before breaking through to become one of the world's most famous abstractionists.

Structures and routines can become false gods created by a society that sees God and Truth as external to the Self. The self-realizer gains the confidence to shatter the restrictive bonds of conformity and assumes the freedom to be unconventional. The psychologically healthy individual in contact with the authentic Self doesn't desire to be like everyone else nor intentionally try to be different.

The authentic person understands that identity depends neither on being separate from nor on being the same as others, as well as understanding that identity is unrelated to the Identifictions of positions or possessions.

Once the truth of the authentic Self is accepted, there is no need for outside confirmation; nor is there need to stand above or apart from the crowd or to acquire control over others. The understanding is gained that nothing is something in the sense that relinquishing self-importance, and the attachment to the Super Me, fosters identity with the greater Self of all humankind. The belief in the metaphysical and spiritual equality of selves erases the need to rise above others or to be like others in order to be accepted.

CHAPTER 8

BARRIERS AND BOUNDARIES

Over many eons, species evolution has depended on protecting separation. People surround themselves with boundaries to protect their family, tribe or nation but also to protect Identifictions and psychological and personal space.

Much of life on both the conscious and subconscious levels deals with maintaining defenses against threats of all kinds—foreign and domestic. All of our lives we have been put on guard to protect life and limb, identity and reputation. The list of threats is endless. We must guard person and property against everything ranging from robbers to rodents, from disease viruses to computer viruses. Last but certainly not least, the most elaborate defenses of all are constructed to protect the ego. Everything is out to get us, or so it seems.

Boundaries between self and other are a huge deal; life, and existence itself, is pretty much all about constructing barriers and boundaries, and then much time and effort is wasted on their maintenance. Children are taught to lock doors at night, and not to trust strangers. As adults we guard against identity theft with secure passwords. The internet is scanned for blogs, sites, and meet-up groups that confirm and reinforce our fenced-in position.

Everything different and external to self is a potential threat to identity—different ideas, races, genders, social positions, religions, interests, you name it. If you are a Christian, you might be a Methodist, whereas I am a Baptist. Even if we are both Baptists, you might be a Southern Baptist, while I am a Reformed Baptist. We both like music, but what do you see in country or rap music?

Problems and conflicts that affect nations and individuals arise from the instinct to protect and defend Positions and Possessions as if the very self were under attack. Countless millions have been the unfortunate victims of wars caused by attempts to either extend or defend national boundaries often coupled with the intolerance of differences. Civilization suffers in so many ways because of the inflated egos of political leaders who, like all of us only more so, believe that meaning and self-realization are found by looking outward, acquiring things, and by taking rather than giving.

However, sometimes, when communication and connections fail to achieve the desired result, barriers and boundaries must be constructed. Lives are endangered by criminals and thugs and the money changers still must be thrown out of the temple. Just as the body's immune system fights off invading germs and the cells of organisms have protective walls, so it is wise to lock doors at night. To live in this material world of separation and duality, it is essential to know where something ends and something else begins, like my nose and your fist.

Obviously, boundaries are necessary, if there is only unbounded oneness, then there is really nothing, no life, no death, no this, no that, but we often go to extremes in building and protecting boundaries, just as we sometimes go to extremes in breaking them down. We over-generalize threats and don't know when to let down our guard. Legitimate defense mechanisms become distorted to create the egocentric feeling that we are in the center of a universe that should only pay attention to our selfish needs in one particular time and place. Fences are built around yards and door locks are installed to protect personal property from outside threats, to protect the self, elaborate ego defenses go up.

At times, the other is us—the objective, superficial self that is filled with Identifictions and does dumb things and believes dumb things just to fit in. This unpredictable, superficial self often builds barriers to protect itself from the threat of being exposed as a fake by the authenticity of the subjective Self. As the old cartoon character Pogo said, "We've met the enemy and he is us."

To protect the value and security of this fragile and phony self, not only is a sense of personal and physical distance established between self and other, but psychological barriers are constructed between the authentic Self and the inauthentic self. Naturally, there is the fear of losing the things that constitute this other self whose identity seems to depend on Positions and Possessions. But it's not just things that are accumulated as part of identity—mental positions are established as an identity, such as being a Christian or an Atheist, conservative or liberal. And so the superficial self as an object is riddled with anxiety and fear because Positions and Possessions can be lost, stolen, or forgotten and belief systems can be attacked and knocked down.

Ironically, the struggle to protect mind and body brings on the very conflict, anxiety, and frustration one seeks to avoid, and this fear frequently underlies the prejudice, fears, and anger directed toward others. Often, an overactive defense system is transformed into an offensive system that can lead to high blood pressure, paranoia, and disease, just as an overly defensive, paranoid nation destroys the liberties of its citizens and attacks nations that are seen as threats.

The more advanced the civilization, the more numerous and varied are the differences between self and other and the greater the number of threats to personal identity. Defenses and protective boundaries become ever more elaborate as civilization advances and population increases. Increased wealth along with decreased personal and physical space calls for more protection and hence isolation from the other.

The disappearance of the front porch on American homes is an indication of how advancing civilization has disrupted connections between self and other. The front porch served as an outside family room where children played, teenagers smooched, parents gossiped with neighbors and grandparents just rocked and watched. Being on the porch was an indication that the family was temporarily lowering its boundaries, an invitation to the neighborhood that the family was open to interacting. With the arrival of the automobile, television and computer, families began staying inside or going for drives. The sense of community drastically declined. Families stopped taking evening strolls in the neighborhood, the front porch was traded for the attached garage. Families could move away from hometowns where they worked and shopped and grew up. The automobile brought tremendous freedom—people moved more frequently, changed jobs more often, could live farther away from home and work, social networks expanded but connections with friends and community became more shallow and tenuous. With the advent of the computer, there is now even less need to socialize.

In a culturally and ethnically diverse country such as the United States, people may seek isolation from foreign elements and look for the comfort and security of their own tribe. Segregation fosters harsher judgements, polarization arises in religion and politics, terrorist attacks increase in conjunction with the increase in distrust and paranoia while empathy decreases. The instinct to preserve and defend separation, when expressed in the extreme as so often is the case, thwarts the cooperative attitude necessary for the smooth and peaceful functioning of an increasingly complex and interdependent world. Developed nations may see an increase in the rise of populist nationalist leaders.

Technologically advanced civilization finds us placed in bubbles isolated from other people and from the demands of communal living. Consequently, families have fewer children, marriages occur less frequently, and personal relationships are less personal and more virtual. "Just send a text, don't call" is a way to avoid the hassles and inefficiencies of in-person communication. People in technologically advanced civilizations not only are walled off from other people, they become increasingly isolated from their natural environment by living, working and driving in climate-controlled houses, cars and work places.

Now don't get the idea that I'm some sort of Luddite who opposes technological innovation but the digital age does have a dark side. In some ways, the computer and the World Wide Web may actually impede the evolution toward unity consciousness and connections with the other. Since digital communication primarily involves only the mind, social interactions become virtual rather than actual. Face-to-face interaction suffers when you reach out and touch someone only with the mind. Graduates today are less interested in attending high school reunions than they were in the pre-digital days because classmates keep updated by means of Facebook. Dinner table, coffee shop, and barroom encounters are disrupted and actually prevented because so many patrons are attached to their digital devices. Why waste time on social niceties like "How are you and how is the family?" when all you really want to know is the time and place of the meeting? And why have a face-to-face meeting when you can have a virtual meeting? Talking is for old fogies; just send a text. The only conversation I now have seems to be with the voice recognition software on the other end of the phone line. I want to see your face, react emotionally to your smile, shake your hand and not just bump fists, which is becoming the substitute for shaking hands. The unity experience involves unity of both mind and body.

Although social media and the internet in many ways do overcome barriers, enhance connections and help to maintain links with vast numbers of friends and relatives, there is a downside. Sara H. Konrath of the University of Michigan has reported that 75 percent of today's college students rate themselves as less empathetic than students of thirty years ago. Jean Twenge, associate professor of psychology at San Diego State University, found that two-thirds of 1,068 students admitted that their generation was more self-promoting, narcissistic, overconfident, and attention-seeking than previous generations, in large part due to their preoccupation with posting on social networking sites. "Selfie," the term used to describe a photograph taken of oneself, was recently added to the lexicon of new words.

The Information Age puts an incomprehensible amount of data and information instantly at the fingertips of anyone with an internet connection. Obviously this is a good thing for the advancement of knowledge. However, as with anything, the human tendency to become immersed in one's personal interests can lead to an unbalanced and distorted world view. Blogs and websites that appeal to every conceivable interest or perversion abound. People become addicted to special interest websites that reinforce and confirm their own positions as the cyber world becomes the real world. Globalization and the internet have increased interconnections but they may also be causing people to cling to the security of smaller identities.

The internet provides an example of the conflict of contact. Although internet access and social media in totalitarian countries has exposed citizens to ideas of freedom and equality, it has often placed them in dangerous conflict with authorities. Progress and change cannot occur without connections, but watch out, for the two cannot completely become the one. The coin will always have two sides.

Now for the good news. Today's new world, with its vastly improved communications and connections, has also brought down barriers and boundaries. Connections are increasing as the world grows smaller and nationalities mix with better and faster communication and more frequent travel between nations. I believe that the adverse impact of the conflict of contact will be lessoned as diverse individuals come to know each other on a personal level.

Boundaries and barriers are coming down. Connections between people and nations and respect for individual rights can happen only in an atmosphere that allows a maximum of conscious and physical freedom. Evidence of freedom's gradual victory is being seen in the political realm, which can set the stage for improved interrelationships between citizens. In 1992, democratic governments finally outnumbered dictatorships. According to a Pew Research Center survey conducted in 2016, the number of democracies among the world's governments has been on an upward trend since the mid-1970s. The average number of democracies in the 1950s was thirty-six; in 2016 the number increased to 97. According to Freedom House, there were 69 electoral democracies in 1990, in 2018 there were 123. As I write this, Pakistan's leader has become the nation's first president in sixty-five years to complete a full five-year term, as I edit this some years later, Indonesia, the world's most populous Muslim nation, has just sworn in its first president who came from outside the military, corporate, or political elite.

Currently the world is enjoying the longest stretch of peace without a major power war since the era of the modern state system nearly five hundred years ago, though, unfortunately, the many terrorist attacks and the rise of nationalism are a disruption to this story. The interdependence fostered by the free flow of goods and services between nations have not only made war less likely, but the benefits from freer trade have enabled hundreds of millions of people to leave poverty and misery behind during the last few decades. As the diverse people of the world bring their established traditions and religions in close proximity to the people of their new world, conflicts will inevitably arise but eventually similarities trump differences.

The hunger for freedom, rooted in the desire for the unity of connections, the urge to merge, eventually wins out over the rigid boundaries of repression and authoritarianism—providing humankind doesn't first self-destruct in the attempt to break the boundaries. Citizens in totalitarian nations want the same freedoms that are available in democratic countries, and they are willing to do almost anything to get it. The problem is that since the mind has evolved very little since Paleolithic times, the new orders are often run by another group of unenlightened leaders who are driven by the same selfish needs for power and self-aggrandizement. Yes, humans want to be free, but boundaries of one kind or another that offer addictive security are likely to rise again in a different form no less exclusive than before.

Worldwide tolerance of diversity is increasing in spite of a setback caused by millions of refugees from Mideast conflicts seeking safety in other countries. Women, gays, and racial and religious minorities are gaining equal rights; even animals have gained certain rights that humans did not have not long ago. The United States elected a black president in 2008, Colorado elected the nation's first openly gay and Jewish governor, and there are now two Muslims in the United States Congress. A multi-nation Gallup International Poll conducted in 2017 found the majority of people and more than half of the 66 countries surveyed say there's no such thing as racial, religious or cultural superiority. According to a 2013 Gallup Poll 87% of 4000 Americans approve of marriage between blacks and whites, and the number increases to 97% for 18–29 year-olds. In 1998, black-white marriages were favored by 64%, compared to a mere 4% in 1958. A 2017 national survey by Pew Research found that 62% of Americans approve of gay marriage, an increase of 14% since 2010.

The big happy group is getting larger and more inclusive. The Pew Forum on Religion and Public Life conducted a survey[1] of 35,000 Americans, which revealed an increasing trend toward tolerance. Sixty-seven percent of American Christians agreed that "many religions can lead to eternal life."[2] An increasing number of Americans, now one in five, are not affiliated with any church or religion—that number increases to three in five in Germany—yet the vast majority of Americans still claim to be spiritual. Pew research data shows that more Americans are registering as Independents,[3] who tend to choose candidates on the basis of their merits rather than on blind adherence to party loyalty, which contradicts the popular notion that the nation is becoming more polarized. Racial differences are also becoming less important. As of 2015, 17 percent of newlyweds were between mixed-race spouses, up from 8.4 percent in 2010, and up from 5 percent in 1980.[4]

---

[1] Pew Research Center 2014 *US Religious Landscape Survey*, June-Sept. 2014

[2] Pew Research Center *Many Americans Say Other Faiths Can Lead to Eternal Life* Dec 18, 2008

[3] Pew Research Center, *5 facts about America's political independents*, July 5, 2016

[4] Pew Research Center *Intermarriage in the U.S. 50 Years After Loving v. Virginia*, May 18, 2017

People all over the world are being brought closer together. Citizens of many nations are being connected by the internet, social media, cell phones, satellite television, air travel, free trade agreements and the European Union. As people come together, not only do they see a commonly shared human nature, but they also become aware that human and environmental problems transcend physical borders. Closer relationships between nations have generated interest in learning about the cultures and languages of other nations. The new emphasis on international relations is especially evident in academia as increasing numbers of students see themselves as global citizens; many US graduate schools offer dual or joint degree programs with international universities; hundreds of thousands of American students spend part of their college years studying in a foreign country and increasing numbers of foreign students study at American colleges and universities.

"Men are driven by two principle impulses, either by love or by fear," according to Niccolo Machiavelli and the result is that we are faced with the great human dilemma of when to open and when to close protective boundaries. The survival of the human race depends more than ever on the individual, society and nation avoiding extremes and knowing when to lower boundaries to let the other in. The challenge is great since not only do boundaries take on so many forms—physical, social, psychological, legal, and now, digital, but there are so many times when boundaries are essential.

CHAPTER 9

COMPETITION, CONFLICT, AND REBELS

Boundary Breakers and Leaders

Human progress always starts with ideas and acts of individuals who break away from the majority opinion or practice.

—Vervon Orval Watts, Tom's father

In 2007 I attended a free rock concert at San Francisco's Golden Gate Park celebrating the fortieth anniversary of the Summer of Love. A few remaining members of old music groups and some good cover bands brought back fond memories of The Mamas and the Papas, Country Joe and the Fish, The Jefferson Airplane and other bands from the 60s. The atmosphere was quite different from that of the year being celebrated. I have fond memories of the communal spirit and feeling of togetherness that permeated the be-ins and festivals of 1967. Conga lines weaved in and out among the crowds of dancers, everyone moved and danced. I contrasted that with the 2007 version of the Summer of Love's crowd that lacked openness and spontaneity, and who protected the boundaries of their little plot of well-defined space with blankets and lawn chairs. There were no conga lines; the dancers occupied a small space near the stage. Gone was the communal spirit and youthful spontaneity that disregarded strict psychological and physical boundaries.

Yes, there are legitimate reasons in this case to protect and reserve a space. From the sanctity of their protected space, the family can enjoy the festival without worrying about being trampled by the ever-encroaching masses. And masses there were—the crowd at the polo fields was estimated at 70,000. The family is protected by the physical boundary of the blanket, just as a country seeks protection by establishing its national borders and an organism survives by maintaining a certain physical separation from its environment. But as so often happens, we can get into a rut, generalize, and go to extremes. The blanket becomes an extension of the owner's identity and anyone who steps on it is actually stepping on the owner.

At times during the festival, boundaries were unintentionally broken. A baby would crawl from one blanket to another, and a dog would wander off its owner's blanket in search of a few leftover picnic tidbits. The uninhibited explorations of babies and dogs provided a socially accepted excuse for the festival-goers to interact as the finder talked with the owners of the baby or dog. The context of the situation had changed, but how unfortunate that an excuse or accidental situation was necessary to open the context for social interaction to take place. So often barriers come down only when situations become extreme, but when engaging in social interaction without waiting for the appropriate context, one risks ostracism, condemnation, or worse. However, when the movers and shakers that lead social and technological change become the initiators of context, boundaries are rearranged.

These thousands of people at the festival, all separated by physical boundaries and boundaries of tradition and culture, all strangers, shared the same inner truth. Sharing this common light can be a very powerful force for good—destruction of boundaries often has a positive outcome. The festive atmosphere can be enhanced if the boundaries of the blanket are broken as the crowd unites to form a conga line or two families join in a communal dance of joy. The Polarity Paradox has been temporarily resolved.

A crowd contains the power and energy of unity, which can be used either constructively or destructively. There is definitely the risk of misusing this power. The possibility of conflicts arise when boundaries come down. The music festival can become a communal love fest as people come together, but out-of-control crowds can also explode into violent, destructive chaos.

Conformity and convention are shallow, stifling, politically correct, and very boring. Charismatic boundary breakers, shake up the status quo and free us from the confines of convention and the prison of conformity that inhibit authenticity and actualization of full potential. This freedom provides an intoxicating burst of energy that can lead to revolution and transformation. The energy, emotional release, and freedom to get in touch with fundamental drives and concerns can become more important than the religious or political message. Mass protests, rallies, and celebrations offer excuses to express deep-seated, pent-up feelings stifled by conventions and conformity.

Unfortunately, this talent for transformation can be used for destructive purposes. Jesus and Martin Luther King Jr. energized crowds, but so did Hitler. The powerful gift to connect with the other is often abused. Some politicians may owe their position to a natural talent for connecting with others but then exploit this desirable gift for personal gain. Perhaps, when Jesus allegedly was tempted by the devil before he began his ministry, it may have been because he was aware of how his profound understanding of Self and other could be used to acquire women, riches, and personal power. Nowadays, rather than the devil, the temptress is the natural human affinity for power and recognition, but advanced understanding can lead to greater riches than could ever come from the acquisition of Positions and Possessions; the profound understanding that truth of Self is truth of other grants unimaginable powers.

The dangerous boundary breakers, the religious and political extremists and demagogues, release a torrent of destructive rather than constructive energy, which perverts or hides repressed desires and identity. As Rollo May, the influential existential psychologist explained, "Since the rebel gets his sense of direction and vitality from attacking the existing standards and mores, he does not have to develop standards of his own. Rebellion acts as a substitute for the more difficult process of struggling through to one's own autonomy."[1]

Caution must be exercised when challenging the current order. Whenever old paradigms are disrupted, society and the individual suffer unintended consequences. There is fierce resistance to the destruction of old boundaries. Traditional ways and beliefs and secure identities are threatened and conflicts erupt between individuals and within nations as diverse groups come into contact. Ethnic and religious groups, pressure groups, moneyed interests, politicians, and the philosophically unsophisticated will clash. There will be backlashes. As one wall comes down, another will pop up.

Fear and anxiety often surface as personal or national Identifictions are threatened and even stricter protective walls of dogmatism and authoritarianism surface. Boundary breakers who pose a threat to moral or social stability, such as Jesus, Martin Luther King Jr., Mahatma Gandhi, Socrates, and Spinoza, incur the risk of certain ostracism, incarceration, or assassination by those who uphold the status quo. But unfortunately, the new order often becomes just as repressive as the old—human nature is slow to change. But there is always hope—humans intuitively know what is right and intuitively tend to follow the dictates of nature's evolutionary course, though often blindly and in fits and starts.

The enlightened boundary breaker advances evolution by courageously facing the lonely task of challenging the status quo. Evolution depends on disrupting the status quo. However, the disruption is often minimal due to the fact that realizing the authentic Self leads to a profound communication resulting in trust based on mutual understanding at the deepest level. Highly successful leaders are effective not because they stand above and apart from others, but because they have the

---

[1]   Rollo May, *Man's Search For Himself*, 1953

ability to form connections with those "under" them and those with whom they disagree, as well as with their "superiors." Reconciling differences depends on understanding similarities between Self and other while at the same time not blessing one and damning the other. A champion athlete, a successful businessman, or your everyday Joe Blow must see a worthy opponent not as an enemy but as an ally who spurs them on to reach their full potential.

We all know of individuals who seem to get along with anyone, regardless of differences in race, gender, religion, politics, or social standing. Think of the people for whom you have great affection, people you like to be around because they make you feel good. You feel completely comfortable and relaxed in their presence. When you are in their presence they give you their complete attention, and may give you the somewhat uncomfortable feeling that they can see right into the depths of your soul because they know you better than you know yourself. They know you because they know themselves, knowledge of other depends on knowledge of Self. In their presence you feel totally accepted and validated.

They accept your failings because they see how your failings are similar to their own. They like you because they like themselves. You want what they have. You want this same confidence in the value of Self. You want to feel this good about who you really are, and you want to feel this good about the other. You want assurance that your path will get you where you want to go, and you want to know where you want to go. Wise leaders know their path, and you want to follow because their path seems perfect. Faith in absolute goodness makes it possible to love the enemy, to be all forgiving, to love neighbor and Self.

The enlightened make you feel needed and important. They need you and benefit from your presence and friendship as much as you benefit from theirs because you are both one person holding different perspectives of the same truth. Having given up Identifictions, they can identify with you. Very simply, I feel good if I accept my Self, but I feel that much greater if I accept you and include you as part of who I am. But here one has to be careful, for it is all too easy to derive false, egotistical pleasure from joining one group to the exclusion of others.

The enlightened boundary breaker makes you feel important by understanding that self-identity and worth depends on opening up to the perfection of the other. But we get this wrong by thinking that perfect Self-identity depends on the relative imperfect identity of the other. Recognizing that the most positive aspects of human nature—compassion, empathy, love, forgiveness, humor—are shared by all enhances authentic identity and leads to the expansive Self we all desire that includes the other.

In the beginning stages of human development, to know and to protect my place, I need boundaries to separate you from me, but to progress toward a higher stage of expanded consciousness and to know you I must step outside the confining boundaries formed by attachments to Positions and Possessions. Although spiritual gurus so often advise us to experience "the power of now" by becoming immersed in the present, the wonder of human nature to consciously transcend the boundaries of space/time allows for the escape from Identifictions that impede connections with the other. This ability to step out of the moment, to leave the false self behind allows one to step into the shoes of the other, to love and understand the other, and to develop the capacity for empathy and compassion.

Winning friendship requires the humble act of lowering the defensive walls of the ego that separate Self from other. Forming close personal relationships entails showing genuine interest in and empathy for the other, listening to the other's troubles and triumphs, seeing their victories and defeats as yours as well and perhaps heeding Emerson's advice that "the only way to have a friend is to be one."

Being on the same level as everyone, notions of self-importance slip away and the other is elevated to a position of supreme importance. The acceptance and respect of others is gained as self-importance is lost.

The self-realized person views the truth from the other's perspective, knowing that the wider the perspective, the greater the understanding of Truth. No matter whether president or stay-at-home parent, the enlightened person is a uniter searching for the common ground. The president agonizes over the fate of the nation's soldiers going to war while the parent agonizes over the dangerous threat to life and limb posed by the daughter's desire to own a motorcycle. The experience and the lesson learned are very similar. The President agonizes over a bankrupt nation, the parent worries about mortgage foreclosure on the family home. Who is to say that the agony of one is greater than the agony of the other? Solutions to problems also have a common ground, as both cases require tense negotiations and living within one's means by sacrificing present pleasures for future gains. The enlightened centered view is aware of the common foundation on which to begin negotiations or build friendships and relationships, and is able to do so without harboring resentment or casting blame.

Since the enlightened understand that the truth of one is truth for all, they are less likely to render criticisms or judgments because by doing so, they criticize themselves. Being able to see through Identifictions enable the boundary breakers to know that the truth of their inner Self is the same as yours. However, if they do criticize you, the criticism is accepted because you understand that their well-intentioned, non-judgmental suggestions help you become the person you want to be, the person you both want to be. Their criticism is accepted because the two of you have formed such a close bond that, to one degree or another, any weakness of one is shared by the other. Disagreements over religion or politics lack the typically accusatory and angry tone usually heard and instead become an elevated discussion of the human role in the universal game of existence.

With the loss of attachments to Identifictions, the distance between Self and other is decreased, making it easier to resolve opposites by encouraging empathy. In the business world, to understand market demand, the entrepreneur must identify with the position of the customer. In politics, a good example of empathy was demonstrated during the 1992 presidential debate between Ross Perot, Bill Clinton, and George H. W. Bush when a member of the audience asked Bush, "How has the recession personally affected you?" Bush's awkward response, "Of course you feel it as president, and that's why I'm trying to do something about it," showed a lack of personal connection, though Bush was considered to be a highly personal individual. Clinton, a masterful politician who understood the importance of personal connection, walked up to the questioner, looked her in the eye and asked, "Tell me again how it's affected you?" Resolving the paradox of polarity lies with understanding what it means to die to live. The ego of the Super Me, which we are most afraid of losing, is the very thing we must lose in order to allow for the connection that unites Self and other. "He must increase but I must decrease" (John: 3:30).

These inspirational leaders, having identified the barriers to unity and authenticity, draw us closer to empathy and love, the highest human emotions that lead to the truth of being that is found by connecting with the other. This centered alignment with universal order, free of Identifictions, permits the mind to penetrate the confusing sea of symbols and conventions that impede human progress and so frustrate and inhibit the creative mind.

Understand that in reality there is no evil. Evil and misfortune are simply problems created by circumstances that must be dealt with in the same way that you put on a coat when it is cold and shorts when it is warm. If your house falls off a cliff, it isn't due to God punishing you for some evil act, but because the house was built too close to the edge. If you break a law, whether civil or spiritual, you pay the fine and suffer the consequences, but you are not evil.

By losing ego attachments, one discovers that true identity is detached from Positions and Possessions. Detachment from Identifictions is a desirable quality in anyone, but especially in a leader. Unfortunately, heroic figures in films and popular culture are often portrayed as having an unrealistic detachment from emotion and passion for anything other than their own oversized ego.

In this dog-eat-dog world, the truly wise person may not get far in the world of politics or business. Moderation is a virtue held by many, but moderation and the middle way energize and excite only the remnant. Nations and the business world are often governed by extremist leaders who have compromised their authenticity by appealing to the biases and prejudices of the masses.

Every once in a while, one person out of many billions, perhaps a Jesus or a Buddha, comes close to breaking through to the next stage of evolution. These individuals, having experienced the unity of knowing the equality of opposition, have realized the authentic Self. But even these rare advanced souls do not have the absolute answer as long as they reside in this material world of limitation. Buddha said that suffering is the nature of existence, and Jesus cried out to God, "Why hast thou forsaken me?" Even if they did have the answer, words and logic could not be used to transmit what can only be experienced. But subconsciously, intuitively, beyond the symbols of actions and language, we sense that the answer is contained in the moment of the process. We are already part of this perfect, special process. Realize, appreciate, and wonder at this fact.

Evolution Depends on Conflict

The comfortable order of the status quo must be disrupted for evolution to occur, whether that evolution is spiritual, physical, organic, or societal. Conflict, fear, and violence often accompany evolutionary progress as the disruption of the status quo is fought and resisted. However, rather than being destructive, the result of contact between extremes can result in the birth of a new order characterized by personal, economic, or societal breakthroughs—providing the disruption is followed by reconciliation. The greater the difference between polarities, the more violent the disruption, but the greater may be the change. The most momentous reaction to change in the orderly status quo was when the Great Cosmo exploded with a Big Bang when its singularity was disrupted to create a universe.

The universe was born in violence and conflict. The death

throes of exploding stars produce the supernovae that give birth to the formation of the elements that contribute to the birth of new stars, planets, and organic life. The higher the initial energy of this process, the more particles are created. The earth's violent collisions with meteors and asteroids led to the extinction of dinosaurs, allowing for the eventual evolution of the human race. Nuclear explosions within the sun produce the atomic fusion that provides the earth with the light and warmth required for the formation of life. In the physical world, conflicting forces may be positive and negative nuclear charges, or the collision of matter and antimatter, or the forces of expansion and contraction. In the biological realm, conflict is waged between one species and another, or between bacteria and viruses struggling for survival in competition with the host organism.

Conflicts between labor and management, or between the oppressed and the oppressor, resulted in the passage of major civil rights legislation, the minimum wage, the forty-hour work week, health benefits, child labor laws, and the right to vote. A cohesive nation may endure many conflicts or outright civil wars in order to stay together. A parent does an unruly child no favors by caving in to unreasonable demands in order to keep the peace; neither does a president promote unity, peace, and harmony by caving in to unreasonable demands of the legislature or media. If the League of Nations had taken a firm stance toward Japan's invasion of Manchuria in 1931 rather than seeking to avoid conflict, or had Neville Chamberlain not followed the path of appeasement in dealing with Hitler in 1938, WWII may never have happened and fifty million lives worldwide may have been saved. But then the pendulum swings too far as the human tendency to see things in the extremes of black and white kicks in. The formerly oppressed now become the oppressors, and conflict again results when skyrocketing pensions and wages cause bankruptcy, or when privileges are granted according to factors other than merit.

Why do so many well-intentioned revolutions fail? The revolutions themselves are often based on freedom and equality, but the revolutionary leaders, as well as their followers, lack the perspective that allows for the breaking of attachments to defensive, egocentric views that pit Self against other. Revolutionary leaders, guided by shallow, black-and-white tunnel vision and still suffering from the us versus them Neanderthal mentality, fail to see the higher truths of conflict resolution and reconciliation.

Hegel famously stated that any given phenomenon contains within itself contradictory aspects that require a movement toward resolution. We desperately seek tranquility and security while at the same time pursuing the excitement and stress that comes from new experiences. Anything that exists not only experiences conflict and tension between opposing forces but also resistance to change. Evolution, progress, and change in the status quo arise out of disorder with the shattering of boundaries and convention and the collision of opposing forces. Creative destruction applies to all levels of society, economics, the arts, sports, science, and politics, as well as to the physical and biological realms.

Competition Aids Survival

Free enterprise, though often maligned by spiritual seekers of unity, offers testimony to the possible benefits of competition and conflict. Capitalism is based on two assumptions; people are governed by self-interest, and when individuals are free to follow their own interests not only does their own condition improve, but the condition of the greater whole benefits as well.

The beauty of free enterprise is that it uses human selfishness, or perhaps we should say self-interest—a natural and desirable trait that can work to the detriment of civilized society—and turns it into a positive force to improve the lives of the collective. Free enterprise also demonstrates how competition and conflict can be used to the advantage of economic development. Since capitalism can't thrive in isolation but depends on a strong family, civic associations, good schools, and democratic governments, the universal law of connections also comes into play.

However, any system or game requires that rules be followed.

Nature sees to it that a higher order natural law, like the "invisible hand" referred to by eighteenth-century Scottish economist Adam Smith, is always operating regardless of human attempts at regulation. But just as we fight the unrestrained natural forces that lead to disease and disaster, so human society is aware that unrestrained self-interest and unregulated capitalism can lead to monopolies, price gouging, low quality, and worker exploitation. Truth carried to extremes becomes falsehood, so, as with any system or game and in the interests of justice, certain boundaries and restraints must be instituted. But as always, due to the inertial tendency to go too far either in regulating or deregulating, a constant readjustment is necessary.

The competition for survival between organisms increases the strength and vitality of the competitors. Competition between groups leads to more cooperation within the group. In the economic sphere, society benefits with better and cheaper products and more jobs as a result of competition. One of the benefits of competition is realized when opponents are seen not as enemies but as partners in the shared pursuit of realizing human potential. Tim Galloway, in his book *The Inner Game of Tennis*, says that when competitors exploit their opponent's weakness, they are actually helping the opponent to get better. Constant tension exists between Self and other in the struggle to "win" the life game against people or situations that interfere with established goals, but humanity is diminished by obsessing with the final score, with the product to the exclusion of the process, and by forgetting that life can be played like a game—identity and personal worth don't depend on winning.

The ground squirrels on the hill behind my house are constantly terrorized by hawks, but in their struggle to survive, the squirrels become faster, healthier, and smarter. In the competitive world of a free market, better and cheaper products are produced for the benefit of the consumer by allowing the less efficient and less creative enterprises to fail. Often more is learned from losing than from winning; the loser benefits by studying the success of the winner. Human potential is realized not by competing against the weak, but by being challenged by the strong.

The benefit of competition is that comparing and measuring one's present position with the positions of others shows that we are capable of becoming more than we ever thought possible. After retiring, to postpone the inevitable physical decline, I began doing push-ups on a regular basis. I thought I was doing pretty well for an old man until I visited a retired friend who, in spite of being 70, five years my senior, could do seventy-five push-ups to my fifty. Having a competitive nature, on arriving home, I surprised myself by doing sixty-two. Comparing our position with that of another can raise expectations and spur us on to more fully realize potential in all areas.

Humans thrive on competition and conflict. Movies, novels, and life itself would be pretty boring without bad guys and adverse situations. Without resistance, muscles atrophy; without challenging the mind, the brain turns to mush. The process of natural selection in which only the fittest survive is at times heartless and cruel as we are witness to the extinction of the weak and the collapse of noncompetitive industries, but the fantastic adaptability of the human species, and of all other life forms, attests to the success of competition. Now, don't get me wrong. Not being a heartless and cruel sort, I do think some sort of safety net is essential for those unable to work.

Opposing forces must be recognized, accepted at some level, and worked with. The devil is here to stay. Recognition, resolution, and reconciliation of the devil and the divine is the name of the game. Civilizations as well as individuals collapse by failing to accept and manage stressful conditions and by refusing to adapt to change.

We may strive for a calm, peaceful, and orderly life, but conflict, tension, and resistance are always present. What may appear calm on the surface hides the turmoil and tumult at deeper levels. I am currently relaxing in the warm comfort of my living room. I look out the window at what appears to be a tranquil scene of rolling green hillsides on a delightfully calm and peaceful day with bright sunshine, a gentle breezes, and a clear blue sky. Yet, on the extreme micro and macro levels, far beyond and beneath what I can sense, there is unbelievable turmoil and violence as subatomic particles are zipping and colliding, neutrinos and photons are traveling close to the speed of light, zillions of bacteria and viruses are attacking organisms, predators and prey are locked in mortal combat, and volcanic furnaces are rumbling in the earth's core beneath where I sit. The violence of nuclear explosions rage within the interior of what appears from my distant perspective to be that calm and orderly star in the sky that bathes this California scene with warmth and tranquility.

Soon I will enjoy the convivial companionship of coffee shop comrades. We will joke and laugh and discuss the current political scene while being unaware of the conflicts boiling and bubbling deep within the subconscious of us all, unaware of the conflicts raging between disparate groups in other nations. But this is not really disorderly chaos, this is supreme, divine order, all part of the plan. Let's get real here. Peace is fragile and often illusory.

The formation and existence of everything from molecules and stars to people and their organizations at times depend on a balance of inward and outward forces, creation and destruction. There is increasing complexity of forms at all levels of existence as molecules form compounds, as singular cells form organisms, and as individuals come together to form tribes and nations. But there is also entropy as systems lose energy, organisms die, civilizations decline and fall, and stars burn and disorganization sets in. But a higher order still operates; the cycle of existence continues as dead stars exploding into supernovas spawn new stars and solar systems, and dead universes may do the same. An evolving universe, just as evolving humans, requires balance, tension, resistance, and conflict between inward and outward forces. However, to avoid stasis and stagnation, often one force, at least temporarily, must exert more force than the other.

A Hassle a Day Keeps the Doctor Away

Letter From the Birmingham Jail

"I have earnestly opposed violent tension, but there is a type of constructive, nonviolent tension which is necessary for growth. Just as Socrates felt that it was necessary to create a tension in the mind so that individuals could rise from the bondage of myths and half-truths to the unfettered realm of creative analysis and objective appraisal, we must see the need for nonviolent gadflies to create the kind of tension in society that will help men emerge from the dark depths of prejudice and racism to the majestic heights of understanding and brotherhood." —Dr. Martin Luther King

Although we usually attempt to avoid stress and conflict, a strong body and mind and even immune system, require a certain amount of stress, and for this reason, humans have a natural urge to seek it out in many forms. According to experts on stress, such as Dr. Ferdaus Dhabhar at Stanford University and Dr. Bruce Rabin at the University of Pittsburgh Medical Center, moderate-exercise stress hormones actually make the brain and body more resistant to psychological stress, and although chronic stress exhausts the immune system and increases blood pressure and heart disease, little bursts of stress ward off infections by strengthening the immune system and may even protect against Alzheimer's. But Dhabhar also emphasizes the importance of allowing sufficient periods of down time between stressful episodes–balancing polarities is always in play.

Humans are complex and confused creatures beset by conflicting drives and needs—tension and relief, solitude and affiliation, order and chaos, freedom and security. The need for a little conflict and tension, the enjoyment of the adrenalin rush, the power of the survival instinct, the thrill of tempting death and flirting with taboos can almost make the devil attractive. We promote love and peace while gawking at car wrecks, watching 300 pound linemen crush football players and pay rapt attention to news stories reporting on terrorist attacks and natural disasters.

Research on mice conducted in 2014 by Vanderbilt Professor Craig Kennedy found scientific evidence for the human craving for violence. The reward pathway in the brain of the mouse is thought to be similar to the same pathway in the human brain. Kennedy found that the positive reinforcer dopamine (one of the hormones responsible for the feeling of pleasure) is released when mice engage in aggressive behavior. Unprovoked mice acted aggressively just for the sake of aggression.

Death, conflict, pain, and suffering hold unimaginable fascination. Halloween, with all its frightful, blood-dripping vampires and zombies, is a multi-billion dollar business. We like to be scared.

Newscasts replay scenes of natural disasters, murders, wars, and riots over and over because who wants to watch boring boy scouts helping little old ladies cross the street? We want to see the old lady getting creamed by a Mac truck and then watch the reaction of her daughter as the reporter asks her, "How do you feel seeing your mother flattened like a pancake?" The good weather channel would never make it. Every story has an antagonist, a bad guy, and the badder, the better.

The more civilized a nation, the more it becomes obsessed with a risk-free, stress-free, comfortable lifestyle.

Strong muscles require exertion and stress, yet many schools no longer require physical education. In fact, to avoid injuries and the inevitable lawsuits that follow, many playgrounds have eliminated parallel bars, rings, slides, teeter totters, and merry-go-rounds. Crash helmets are required for bike riding, skateboarding, and skiing. The shot put, discus, javelin, hammer throw, and pole vault have been eliminated from some high school track programs as being too dangerous. Dodgeball is often eliminated from physical education classes because it is said to promote aggression. Some economists think the recovery from the 2008 United States recession took years longer than recoveries from previous recessions because of the government's extensive bailouts in the attempt to prevent economic stress. Wanting to avoid the hassle of raising children, more parents are deciding not to have children.

Contemporary society's obsession with cleanliness has led to an overuse of antibiotic soaps that is creating strains of drug-resistant super bugs. The sterile environment in which today's children are raised results in weaker immune systems that put children at higher risk of developing allergies and asthma.

To avoid conflict and tension, concerns that reach into the very depths of human existence are often avoided. The taboo subjects of sex, politics, religion, and death bring on strong feelings and conflicts that are uncomfortable topics of discussion. These are life's most important concerns, and avoiding these topics makes people as dull and shallow as their conversations. Religion addresses the basic issues of the meaning of life as well as the notions of good and evil. Politics focuses on the basic relationships between the individual and the collective, and is involved in every segment of society. It's pretty obvious that without sex you wouldn't be reading this, and I never would have written it. And forget about death and dying, one of the most taboo subjects of all.

As a result of the taboo against discussing these relevant subjects, little practice is gained in dealing with the natural conflicts and hassles of life. When crucial areas of life are avoided, when needs are unmet and conflicts unresolved, pressure builds up as desires become obsessive, exaggerated and distorted and find expression in undesirable ways.

Naturally death and dying are foreign to the living, but associated thoughts and concerns are increasingly avoided in a contemporary society obsessed with youth and vitality. The old and infirm are kept out of sight and out of mind. In the not too distant past, birth as well as death took place in the home and the sights and sounds and smell and agony of death and the ecstasy of birth were familiar.

The polar extremes of life, birth and death take place in hospitals. Both extremes, the very young and the very old, are tucked out of the way in specialized care institutions. Just as the extreme avoidance of the stress and hassles of life can be destructive to mental and physical health so unfamiliarity with death and dying add to their mystery and increase the likelihood of unnatural reactions—obsessions with gore and violence, avoidance of solitude and quiet, seeking the inclusiveness of group protests and demonstrations as substitutes for close inter-personal relationships.

Both the individual and society are endangered by the failure to find appropriate expression for the "seven sins" listed as anger, jealousy, envy, gluttony, lust, sloth, and pride. Unless the dark side is allowed a safe outlet, conscious or otherwise, one risks letting loose the devil in uncontrolled and destructive ways. Normal desires become distorted into the form of criminal behavior or mental illness. Unnatural and extreme attempts to recapture the adrenalin rush produced by the stress response, or attempts to repress it, are likely to result in an increase in violent, risky, or criminal behavior.

Speed has taken on exaggerated importance. Looking back to my youth, I remember how thrilling it was to ride the old wooden roller coaster at the Santa Cruz Beach and Boardwalk built in 1924, which is still crawling along at a speed of 55 miles per hour. This old coaster ride would put today's kids to sleep, kids who are whipped around and upside down at speeds close to 100 miles per hour on modern coasters. The Formula Rossa in Abu Dhabi accelerates from 0 to a blistering 149 miles per hour in four seconds. In 1960, the highest roller coaster was about a hundred feet; within twenty-five years it had climbed to over two hundred feet, and now the Kingdu Ka at Six Flags in Jackson, New Jersey, towers at a whopping 456 feet. The adrenaline rush is actually an enjoyable high if no real danger is present.

The seven deadly sins, which are anything but deadly, are given somewhat of a bad rap. In fact, they are based on natural human emotions possessing survival value that drive civilization and make humans human. Many extraordinary accomplishments in every field of endeavor can be attributed to these vices. Taking pride in accomplishments, envying another person's positions or possessions, lust for fame and fortune, all of these so-called sins drive the building of great cities, the creation of monumental works of art, and the writing of great novels. Being basically lazy or slothful motivates people to invent labor-saving devices. Without righteous anger, Jesus may not have thrown the money changers out of the temple.

An overly safe world compels its citizens to invent threats and thrills in order to provide the adrenalin rush necessary to recapture the passion of being alive. If we don't have enough conflict and stress, we create our own.

The need grows for ever more stimulation and can often be seen in today's world. As conflicts, risks and tension are avoided, life becomes more unreal and reality shows on television grow in popularity where viewers can see the conflicts they avoid be confronted. Video games and ultimate fighting glorify violence and mayhem; extreme sports like skydiving, bridge jumping, and free-running are gaining in popularity.

It seems that every year movies and television programs depict more gruesome acts of violence. The Lone Ranger, a popular hero in the 1950s, never killed the bad guy, but just shot the gun out of his hand or knocked him cold, all with not a drop of blood being spilled. As I am writing this, one of the most popular TV shows, "The Walking Dead," shows the good guys splitting the heads of zombies, spilling and splashing blood and brains about in every episode.

Evolution requires disruption of established order. Perfect order includes motion and change, and resistance is the natural response to change. Just as the universe howled when its singularity was disrupted and nuclear explosions can result from splitting the peaceful atom, so humans howl in protest when their orderly existence is threatened. The experience of tension, conflict, and resistance is a consequence of being caught in space/time, where one is always lagging just a little behind or jumping a little ahead of the flow of existence. A creature caught in space/time necessarily finds Self alienated from other.

Humans thrive on conflict and tension, yet work so hard to get rid of it. The constant challenge is learning how to deal with conflicts and tension, how to play with the devil. Much benefit can be derived from the stimulating stress-related hormones if stress energy is channeled into productive action. Laughter and sex are so enjoyable because of the contrasting calm that ensues with the release of tension.

The need for extreme experiences may be lessoned by gaining appreciation for solitude and silence through some form of meditation or mindfulness. Take a break, slow down, and appreciate the wide-open, quiet spaces. The key is to find meaning in the off as well as the on. Occasional dwelling in the empty space of silence allows room for the other to enter. Truth requires the experience of conflict and contrast, but remember to release attachment, return to Self, and you will dance with Cosmo. This is the way to the connection between us and God, between Self and other, which I call the Super Connection.

CHAPTER 10

PLAY WITH THE DEVIL

There Is No Evil

"My administration has a job to do, and we're going to do it. We will rid the world of the evil doers." President George W. Bush issued this proclamation five days after the 9/11 attacks and it wasn't long before he gathered the troops to take out the "evil" Saddam Hussein. But bad guys like Stalin, Hitler, and Mao Tse Tung also wanted to cleanse the world of "evil" impurities as do the radical Islamists of today. According to Zen teacher and author David R. Loy, "One of the main causes of evil in the world has been human attempts to eradicate evil. Much of the world's suffering has been the result of our way of thinking about evil." I couldn't agree more.

The Greek term for the universe was kosmos, which means "that which is ordered." Anything that follows this universal order (which I call the Great Cosmo) is perceived of as beautiful and therefore good. Anything that destroys order, or is out of order, might be considered bad or evil. But I contend that existence is as orderly as whatever created the universe. Nothing exists outside of this perfect order; therefore, there is no evil. Imperfection can't come out of perfection. What is considered to be bad or disorderly is defined as such only from the human's limited, finite perspective.

If evil is that which is contrary to or outside of God's control, then God can't be omnipotent and perfect since perfection has no room for the error of evil. If God is love, the ultimate good, then it would be an oxymoron to say that we should love the evil devil, the personification of hate, yet Jesus said to love your enemy. "How can we love that which is opposed to God?" is a meaningless question. Actually, nothing is opposed to God, so there is no evil. In Old and Middle English, evil didn't have the moral or supernatural implications it holds today but simply meant "bad." Evil seems to have Germanic and Greek roots that relate to "up" and "over," connoting extremism.

If there is but one God, and if that God is omniscient, omnipresent, and infinite, it has to incorporate evil into its being. Remember Isaiah 45:7, "I am the Lord . . . I form light and create darkness, I make peace and create evil, I am the Lord, who do all these things." Being associated only with good diminishes God. Loving the creator God requires also loving its destructive aspect.

I am certainly not suggesting that because there is no evil that no judgments should be rendered relative to whether something is good or bad. Nor am I suggesting that we shouldn't work to improve an imperfect world.

Evil is still a useful word. When something absolutely horrendous occurs, such as the slaughter of innocent children, evil seems the appropriate term to describe the event or persons responsible. Good and evil are relative terms, but as long as life is the value, then the standard for good must be whatever encourages optimum life.

The more clearly it can be seen that there is no metaphysical evil force, that lives and choices are governed by the same impersonal yet perfect laws of nature that form and erode mountains, the closer will be the stress-free peace and harmony of the heart's desire. Replace the notion of cosmic evil with the idea that some things are simply out of harmony with cosmic order, and try to understand the natural processes responsible for disharmony.

If lightning strikes a church, it is not the devil's work, nor is

God punishing evil-doers; it is because some idiot forgot to install a lightning rod. The parishioners who believe in evil rebuild the church—again without a lightning rod—after listening to the priest sermonize how disaster wouldn't have happened if they had avoided evil ways.

Cosmo's natural law makes no moral distinction and is not a judge of good or evil. One cannot say that gravity is an evil force because it causes the rock to hit you on the head. The tree with crooked branches and wilted leaves isn't judged to be inferior to the healthy tree; rather, we seek to understand the conditions that are hindering its health, for those very conditions could affect the healthy tree as well. Neither is the person condemned whose life revolves around crime; instead, the causes of the person's behavior are sought in order to prevent others from meeting the same fate. However, just as a contagious person may have to be quarantined, so society must be protected from the criminal.

Life Is the Standard

Once again the problem arises that if all is perfect, then nothing makes any difference and anything goes. The obvious truth is that some times and places are better than others and some things are better than other things—if life is the standard. As I wrote earlier, accepting the perfect moment doesn't mean we should be content to rot away in our easy chairs. We have to get off our butts, exercise, eat right, mow the lawn, earn a living and fight the bad guys.

Rejection of evil and the acceptance of the moment does not imply that no attempt should be made to change circumstances. But to become angry or hateful toward a cup of bad coffee or the manager of the shop is really to be angry at the Great Cosmo that forged the moment. If a rock hits you on the head, it may be natural to let loose a stream of expletives, but after the pain subsides, you don't condemn the rock or hold on to a lingering hate of all rocks as well as the force of gravity. Instead, you wear a hard hat, build a retaining wall, or get the hell out of the way. To the extent that you are angry, intolerant, and impatient with the circumstances of life, to that extent faith in the perfection of universal order has been replaced with the egotistical faith in the separate and unconnected power of the ego-self.

I don't subscribe to the belief that all cultures, all religions or situations are of equal value. If life is the standard, then it only makes sense that the criteria used for evaluating actions or situations is deciding which best provides for optimum physical, psychological, and spiritual welfare of the individual. A way of life that encourages pain, violence, intolerance, or retribution is inferior to one that promotes love, peace, tolerance, and forgiveness.

Play With the Devil

By branding something as evil, a person either consciously or subconsciously elevates himself or herself to the moral high ground and establishes an irrevocable barrier between Self and other. This kind of mental laziness and simplistic, dualistic thinking provides little motivation to look for causes or solutions, since one tends to believe that an evil person is beyond redemption. It is much easier to just execute the bastard, destroy the evil, and be done with it.

Being possessed by devilish negativity is the consequence of wrong attitudes toward evil. Jesus advised, "Love your enemies," which is another way of saying, "Love the devil." Martin Luther King Jr. famously said, "Returning hate for hate only multiplies hate; darkness can't drive out darkness." To prevent the dark side from gaining control, it must first be recognized and then allowed some form of safe expression, something modern society often finds difficult to do.

We have been conditioned to reject the dark side of human nature, the shadowy images that haunt dreams and nightmares, the reservoir of not only all that we fear and hate, but of our fascination with horror and violence, conflict and tension. Carl

Jung referred to this unconscious aspect of human nature as the shadow self.

Optimal health of mind and body depends not only on incorporating the shadow into our lives, but understanding that realizing human potential relies on understanding the roots of our fears—ignorance feeds the devil. The shadow self, the devil within, must be integrated into awareness.

The drive for unity is thwarted by both ignoring and rejecting the shadow. Extreme rejection actually encourages emotional attachment, which allows the devil to gain control. As anger, hate, fear, and guilt flood the brain with negativity, all other thoughts and emotions are pushed aside. If unrecognized or rejected, demons may surface in the extreme form of neurosis and psychosis. By hating—or by too strongly rejecting—the devil, you actually make it stronger.

In order to prevent negative emotions from taking over, invite the devil to play when it first raises its head. We are playing with the devil by laughing at an off-color or harmless practical joke, by enjoying the theatrics of a professional wrestling match, and even by participating in or watch aggressive or violent games, such as football, boxing, or ice hockey. Feelings of resentment, prejudice, anger, and jealousy must be recognized to bring the devil under control.

Sports serve as a microcosm of all the challenges and struggles of life. Involvement in sports either as a participant or as a spectator can serve as a safe and healthy outlet for the shadow self *if sports is seen as a game*. Yet strong team attachment and the failure to recognize the reasons for the allure of sports can increase the devil's influence by intensifying aggressiveness, competitiveness, the drive for power and the desire to win at any cost.

Joining or supporting a team can allay anxieties of feeling alone and separated. As traditional institutions of family and religion break down, team identification takes its place. When personal identity depends on Identifictions, the need to belong, the need to increase self-esteem and self-worth leads us to seek connections with sports teams, religions, nations, clubs or ideologies. However, fanatic sports fans have succumbed to the shadow's drive for power and status and have acquired Identifictions as their personal identity becomes tied to the team. The game of football is no longer seen as a game but becomes a life and death struggle. Relegating competing teams and opposing fans to inferior status leads to tribalism and an us versus them mentality.

A barrier to understanding the enemy, whether within or without, is the fear that any contact with evil will lead to permanent attachment and personal corruption. If I dislike you then it pains me to admit that you have some good ideas. I have put you into a category of opponents and then made the sweeping generalization that everything about you is wrong.

Since we cannot serve two masters, the devil must be released in order to dance with God. By playing Catch and Release, the spiritually advanced soul is prevented from forming attachments to "evil." Since time does not factor into the game, the negative pole can be released at the moment of recognition followed by the return to the center which then makes possible the objectivity and detachment necessary to play and laugh at the devil. In the heat of the game you shout at the umpire, roar with the crowd, yet all the while realizing you're playing along. You lose your temper when that guy cuts you off in traffic, but try the trick of yelling, "Love you, buddy!"

It is at civilization's and humankind's peril to fail to accept and understand the devil that shadows the divine. It has been said that what humans consider to be evil is simply God's shadow. Obliterate the shadow and that which creates the shadow is destroyed. Absolutely condemning the shadow self, failing to see the devil as an aspect of the divine, leads to an uptight and unfulfilled life where love is drowned out by guilt and repression.

Recognizing Extremes

The tendency to go to extremes, and to generalize and simplify, often causes the total acceptance of one side and the total rejection of the other. These tendencies can lead to the disastrous attempt to completely destroy the devil by eliminating all tension, struggle and conflict.

I mentioned in a previous chapter that, in the interests of safety, many playgrounds have eliminated teeter-totters and schools have eliminated certain track and field events. In the interests of peace, cooperation and equality, some well-meaning educators have eliminated all competitive sports and games from their schools. In addition, rather than awarding students for outstanding individual achievement, every student receives an award. Conflict, competition and struggle are not only necessary for optimum health, evolution and survival but are unavoidable.

Failure to deal with the shadow self not only suppresses individualism and authenticity but intensifies and exaggerates the drive for power and status which encourages Identifictions.

Humankind intuitively understands that evil must be avoided while also recognizing that both creative and destructive forces are necessary aspects of universal evolution—the devil, being essential to the divine, is only God being misunderstood.

Recognizing extremes is vital to the evolution of unity consciousness since knowing one extreme can lead to understanding the opposite pole. However, opposition must not only be recognized, opposing sides must in some way be experienced—one must play or joke with the devil to dance with God.

Some people make seemingly miraculous rebounds from lives that at one time were mired in the depths of depravity. A former student of mine became involved in drugs and gangs at the age of fourteen, but after spending a few years in San Quentin, eventually acquired a national reputation for his work in turning kids away from gangs and drugs. Nicky Cruz, a notorious New York City gang leader featured in the book and film *Run, Baby, Run* became the co-founder of Victory Outreach, the well-known Christian ministry that reaches out to help gang members reform their lives. Two of my good friends were high school drop-outs, got in fights and abused drugs, yet went on to graduate from college, become successful professionals, and are two of the most wonderfully generous and caring people you'd ever want to meet. We have all heard stories of people's close encounters with death that resulted in a renewed appreciation and zest for life.

Experiencing the negative pole seems to provide the opportunity to more fully experience the positive. But it may not be the actual experience of one extreme that leads to the understanding of the opposite extreme. It is the *openness* to the extreme that enables one to be open to the experience of the opposite pole. Still, the value in deeply understanding extremes is that it fosters empathy.

Here it is important to emphasize that devilish ways need not be expressed or experienced physically, just as losing attachment doesn't mean physically throwing away prized possessions. I am certainly not suggesting that you act on every extreme thought or join gangs, become drug users, and seek near-death experiences. Obviously, not every gangster, alcoholic, or deprived youngster will make such a turnaround. Just as it is unnecessary to have a close encounter with physical death in order to gain an appreciation for life, neither is it necessary to lead a life of crime in order to have empathy for the criminal. Caution is advised, watch out for attachments since an open mind is open to the guiles of the devil as well as to the glories of the divine.

Pursuing the Perverse, the Devil's Attraction

Humans are curious creatures, so intrigued by the hidden and forbidden and the taboos behind the closed door. In spite of the civilized world's attempt to reject danger, death and destruction, guts and gore, these forbidden demons remain ever fascinating.

It is paradoxical that humans go to such great lengths to avoid conflict and disharmony, yet conflict has such a strong attraction that it becomes part of personal identity, incorporated into the shadow self. Would the Palestinians and Israelis or Democrats and Republicans really be happy with the resolution of their differences? Have you met people who seem to thrive on conflict, who love arguing just for the sake of argument?

Violence, pain, and suffering are feared and rejected while at the same time holding a macabre fascination. The greatest mystery and taboo is death, the ultimate isolation and separation from the material world. Anxieties associated with death are manifested as fears of losing anything to which attachments have been formed, including friends, loved ones, material possessions, tennis matches or fears of isolation and rejection.

Death, as the greatest unknown, becomes the source of life's greatest fear and opposition. The greater the fear, the greater the separation and the stronger the opposition. Humans are attracted to and tempted by opposition.

The survival instinct is the origin of many forces that drive human thoughts and actions, and any obstacle to these drives, to one degree or another, can be seen as an evil force to be overcome.[1] To aid in survival, humans evolved the Will to Unify to connect with something greater than the self such as a group or a tribe but which can also be a God or an ideology.

Feelings of inadequacy or incompleteness drive the need to connect and can also drive what Friedrich Nietzche called the Will to Power. Uniting with a group, and cooperating with its members offers the individual more power and control than is possessed by the individual standing alone. Viktor Frankl's Will to Meaning also contributes to a person's feeling of adequacy and power by driving group membership, the establishment of goals, or dedication to a cause.

Humans want power, either over themselves or over the other (people, situations). Power provides autonomy, value, protection, control and order. If I can't be as powerful as I'd like then at least I want to associate with the powerful, and what is more powerful than God. However, if God is the ultimate in goodness and power then the forces of evil actually seem to be more

---

[1] As I've said before, I don't believe in evil as a supernatural or metaphysical force but it is a useful term

powerful than God.

Humans are intrigued by what appear to be forces powerful enough to disrupt the very order that Cosmo has established. Evil appears as a force capable of actually destroying the order imposed by God and humans, and what is more disruptive to God's order than death, destruction and nonexistence?

To understand and hence manage the devil it is vital to uncover the roots of our own disorder as well as to see the many positive and negative ways these drives and forces are expressed in the struggle to survive. For example, the Will to Power, usually seen in a negative way, can have benign expressions as acts of charity, service, kindness and praise. The Will to Unify, usually thought of in positive terms, can be the driving force to join militant or terrorist groups with the goal of blowing things up which is a negative expression of the Will to Meaning.

In the interests of maintaining order, societal constraints and social pressures bear down from every corner to inhibit and restrain human desires and spontaneity and discourage eccentricity and deviance from the norm.

Feelings of inadequacy and powerlessness arise in part from a society and culture that condemns the shadow by teaching the doctrine of original sin and submission to external authority.

Ignoring societal constraints, criminals, rebels and renegades are often secretly admired as counter-cultural anti-heroes who challenge authority and power structures of an uptight, inhibited and over regulated society that robs the rest of us of power and autonomy. Why else would gangsters and rebels have such a powerful influence on fashion, music and so many aspects of culture? Baggy pants gained popularity from a prison gang phenomenon, the fedora's height of popularity in the 1930's was influenced by Al Capone. The distressed jeans that are nearly ripped to shreds, today's fashion statement, were first worn by the punk culture of the 1970's who tore apart consumer goods as an expression of their anger against a rigidly controlled and authoritarian society.

The first step in defanging and dealing with the devil is to understand its source of power. The devil's power resides in the related human fears of isolation, rejection and separation and in the false notions of what is necessary to allay these fears. Humans are profoundly aware that, as material beings, they have limited power, limited life spans and are doomed to eventual extinction.

The devil's negative power can be transmuted to positive power by understanding what is behind the drives for unification, power and meaning, and by understanding that authentic identity is found by detaching from the Identifictions of Positions and Possessions.

The devil takes many forms but in the form of the Identifictions of Positions and Possessions, it can only be dealt with by a non-defensive openness to understanding how Self and other are one. We can never acquire enough of or the right positions or possessions to satisfy the Will to Unify or to make the Super Connection.

The mind often exaggerates reality, making things either better or worse than they actually are. Imagination takes hold by constantly stepping out of the present into the past or future. Once the striptease dancer is naked, the imagined hidden treasures are revealed and the act is over, the mystery is solved. Familiarity doesn't always breed contempt, but while it may lead to boredom, it can also lead to understanding and loss of attachment. Many marriages are broken up because the mystery disappears, the thrill is gone, and the image is replaced by reality. However, deep understanding and familiarity lead to a deeper, more genuine and authentic love. Knowledge and understanding are synonyms for love, so understand the devil.

There is a natural human desire to defeat the devil by resolving conflict by bringing warring parties together which can transform evil to good. The release of tension is a desired end goal. Although conflict and tension between the forces of good and evil are entertaining and necessary elements for a good story, we are instinctively inclined to want good to win out in the end. Better yet, we like to see evil transformed into good, and it is for this reason *The Christmas Carol*, by Charles Dickens, is so widely popular. It is the classic portrayal of the transformation of evil, in which the cold-hearted, miserly Ebenezer Scrooge is transformed into a generous and joyful benefactor.

Perhaps the destiny of the universe is experienced through fear and anxiety provoked by the awareness of death and finitude. The human tendency to resist destructive forces is a manifestation of matter resisting disintegration in the process of entropy. Humans are the universe being conscious of itself and being in and of the universe, are also subject to entropy, the difference being that we are consciously aware of what is happening and fight and resist what we see as the evil forces that determine our eventual fate. But humankind also shares the nature of the higher order forces of creation that can overcome entropy, the creative forces that bring existence into being and enable us to see beyond the entropy of the mere physical.

The ultimate Super Connection between Self and other is always just a little beyond reach, impeded by the boundaries of a material world that traps humankind in the wake of its own footprints. As long as our consciousness is trapped in a material body in a material world, the Will to Unify will never be completely attained, satisfaction is fleeting, and the devil will always be with us. This is the way it is meant to be. Dissatisfaction keeps us and the universe evolving, changing, reaching and forging new creations. We will never have it all, there is no existence without opposition, which is the human experience of dissatisfaction and desire.

The extent to which Identifictions can be eliminated, to that extent will the opening be created for seeing Self in other. Actually uniting with the other is the unattainable Super Connection but seeing Self in other is the key to dealing with the fears of separation that feed the devil and is key to approaching the Super Connection. The understanding that Identifictions can never be completely eliminated, that separation is literally a fact of life, allows us to play with the devil thus preventing it from getting out of control.

Joke With the Devil

One way to handle the devil is through the use of humor. According to comedians Keegan-Michael Key and Jordan Peele, "The purpose of humor is to help people cope with the fears and horrors of the world." Laughter alleviates tension, destroys boundaries, penetrates symbols, reduces conflict, deals with incongruity and calms the devil.

Comedians are sort of like kung fu masters. The practitioner of martial arts defeats evil by using the power and force of the opponent to his or her advantage. Using almost no force, a master of martial arts can overcome a much stronger opponent. Just as the secret in martial arts is to avoid attachment to the destructive force, so humor can be employed to break attachment to the devil.

Humor blasts categories and conventions by making fun of the discriminating mind's futile attempt to control and confine the infinite with definitions. Humor ridicules the attempt to resolve irresolvable paradoxes. Truths are revealed by destroying the boundaries of stereotypes and political correctness, and by breaking attachments to long-held personal mythologies. A moment of satori is often associated with a burst of cosmic laughter. As Joel Goodman, the famous doctor of humor, said, "There is a connection between HAHA and AHA."

Personal identities are so caught up in Identifictions, and the pursuit of happiness, and meaning is so often misdirected, that it's pretty hard not to expose the absurdities for what they are. However, so-called political correctness is stifling humor to such an extent that many comedians refuse to perform at colleges and universities. The truth can hurt. George Bernard Shaw once said, "If you are going to tell people the truth, you'd better make them laugh. Otherwise they'll kill you." But political correctness is killing the humor that offers a detached perspective that can help us cope with craziness, and serve as a reminder that life is a stage play.

Religion and spirituality are taken too seriously. There is a laughing Buddha, but Jesus, Moses, and Muhammed are rarely thought of as having a sense of humor, and examples of humor in the Bible are hard to come by.

Several research studies confirm that laughter is good for us physically as well as psychologically. Research conducted by Dr. Lee Berk and others at Loma Linda University in California showed that diabetic patients who laughed at a humorous sitcom or video for thirty minutes a day increased their good cholesterol by 26 percent and dropped their level of C-reactive protein, a marker for heart-harming inflammation, by 66 percent. Being uptight, defensive, or hateful causes blood vessels to constrict, which in turn contributes to high blood pressure, strokes, and heart attacks. Conversely, as we relax and become a little less uptight and defensive, our bodies react accordingly and reap the benefits. Laughter has also been found to boost immunity, increase alertness, reduce stress, and benefit heart patients by lowering blood pressure by dilating blood vessels, and as my favorite cosmic comedian, Steve Bhaerman, better known as Swami Beyondananda says, "Laughter causes our blood vessels to dilate, which is better than having them die early." Neuroscientist John Allman from the California Institute of Technology and other researchers found another benefit to humor: it is a whole-brain experience.

Comedy routines in clubs are laced with the frequent use of the forbidden F-word. The therapeutic use of the forbidden was revealed in a recent study conducted at Britain's Keele University, where it was found that the use of the F-word can reduce pain.[2] In this study conducted by Richard Stephens, sixty-four college students immersed a hand in ice water for as long as possible. In one trial, the subjects were allowed to use a curse word of their choice while enduring the painfully cold water, while in the other round, only non-expletives could be issued. It was found that using socially unacceptable swear words not only allowed students to withstand the cold longer but also decreased

---

[2] Stephens Richard, Atkins John, Kingston Andrew *Swearing as a response to pain*, Neuroreport, Aug 5, 2009

their perception of pain intensity.

What is interesting is that Stephens found that cursing reduces pain perception more strongly in women than in men, possibly because men swear more than women in daily life.[3] This study is a good example of the use of Catch and Release: briefly play with the devil, but not too often. Swearing can be useful, but if used too often, it loses its punch, just as comedians lose their effectiveness by overusing the F-word.

"True humor begins when man ceases to take himself seriously," Hermann Hesse wrote in his novel Steppenwolf. And boy, do we take ourselves seriously. Our identity is caught up with so many "things" that it seems there is less and less available to make fun of. This attachment to identity and things causes a lack of awareness since attention is so focused on the object of attachment. People who are preoccupied with themselves are less likely to connect with and appreciate their surroundings. The other will be of interest to the self-attached only to the extent that the other serves the purpose of enhancing Identifictions.

The ultimate state of detachment is when you can laugh at yourself when playing Catch and Release by being a comedian and your own straight man. Self-deprecatory humor is a form of ego death in which you deny the importance of your Identifictions. The enlightened jokesters are aware that the joke is on them, and for this reason, without taking personal insult, a blonde can laugh at a dumb blonde joke, a Jew can laugh at a Jewish joke, and whites can joke about not being able to jump.

Laughing at your own expense immediately puts others at ease. Making light of my problems and weaknesses, some of which are undoubtedly shared in some way by you, enables you to safely bring to the surface your own problems. Denying self-importance leaves room for the importance of others. Earlier I mentioned the miserable woman on my cruise who for a moment was able to laugh at misfortune and, for a while at least,

---

3   Time Magazine, August 10, 2009, p. 57

disarm the devil. The devil is often the inauthentic Identifictions that humor so effectively obliterates.

Humor is the enemy of attachment; it can only thrive in an atmosphere free of control and attachment. It's hard to laugh when you are uptight or filled with hostility. Detachment, increased awareness, and humor are interrelated: the more detached one becomes, the more areas in which humor is seen, and the more aware one is of the surroundings. By exposing taboos and bringing to light forbidden subjects, and by shattering the uptight and politically correct, comedians are the world's greatest therapists. Comedians are equally at home with saint and sinner.

Attachments are hard to avoid, but one solution is to believe in the Equality of Selves—we are no better or worse than anyone else. Understand that to one degree or another all the strengths and weaknesses associated with being human are shared by all. The universal creative order, the Great Cosmo, is an equal opportunity employer who treats all entities equally by raining on the just as well as the unjust. Fight the unjust without being possessed by hate or resentment, toss out the moneychangers, and then move on.

When we relax, when we lose a little control and lose a little attachment, then the important connections will happen as desires and expectations lessen. By embracing our dual nature and understanding the necessity for polar opposites, true self control is gained, extremes of thought and behavior disappear, and the dark side begins to hold less fascination.

To again quote Hermann Hesse on humor: "To live in the world as though it were not the world, to respect the law and yet stand above it, to have possessions as though one possessed nothing, to renounce as though it were no renunciation, all these favorite and often formulated propositions of an exalted worldly wisdom, it is in the power of humor alone to make efficacious."

CHAPTER 11

FREE WILL: MYTH OR REALITY?

At any time I can freely choose to press the delete key, obliterate this entire document, take up violin lessons, and shoot up my neighborhood. Of course, as long as I maintain my sanity, I am not going to make any of these choices, though there are no physical restraints preventing me from doing so. I can come up with any number of reasons why I won't commit these actions, and there are many more factors influencing my actions and thoughts of which I am unaware.

Every day a degree of anxiety is experienced in the face of constant choices between alternative courses of action—should I marry or remain single, should we have children, which candidate is most qualified, do house repairs and upgrades take precedence over funding a vacation, should I vote innocent or guilty? The feeling that I have the freedom to choose is as real as the anxiety it can produce. Survival requires the confidence of being in control of thoughts and actions.

The experience of free will, and the concomitant acceptance of personal responsibility for our choices is vital for the individual and for society. It is practical and expedient to lock up the bad guys and reward the good guys, since the threat of incarceration is a disincentive for criminals, and rewards encourage good behavior. Incentives and disincentives are necessary environmental influences that help determine behavior and choices.

As necessary as the experience of free will is, believing that we are in complete control of thoughts and actions contributes to many of the prejudices and negative attitudes held toward others as well as toward the Self. Many of the judgmental and self-righteous attitudes that interfere with the humility necessary for genuinely connecting with others arise from the belief in free will. Free will advocates are likely to hold the position that social and personal problems, such as poverty, crime, and drug addiction, are simply due to laziness, stupidity, and personal irresponsibility. As an example, many people blame specific groups for crime and terrorist attacks, whereas a determinist puts the blame on human nature and the societal conditions that contribute to the problem. The belief in absolute free will can result in taking too much blame or too much credit for actions and beliefs. However, the extreme determinist may give too little importance to personal responsibility.

The belief in free will causes us to put ourselves on a higher plane by criticizing people for any number of reasons. In an earlier chapter I discussed how such judgments break connections. Many criticisms are valid, but judgments can be transformed into mere observations by remembering that people's actions and thoughts are determined. By not harboring harsh judgments, people who disagree are more likely to calmly reach an agreement. As previously discussed, natural features such as mountains, trees, and oceans are appreciated and accepted without judgments knowing that their formation is caused by immutable and perfect natural laws from which there is no escape. In the same way, the determinist is more likely to be understanding of human imperfection. In neither case are imperfections or problems ignored, it is just that negativity and intolerance have been defanged by a more critical view of free will.

The supremely important ego of the Super Me thinks it is in complete control, free and separate from the Great Cosmo. The wrong assumption here is that human behavior and thought are somehow outside the laws of cause and effect that govern the nonhuman world. This is not to say that events are predictable—there are simply too many variables involved—only that there is no escaping the natural processes that determine thoughts and actions.

A human being is not a prime mover or a cause of its own existence. Every effect has a cause, and every cause has an effect—at least in our world. Meteorologists still can't accurately predict the weather, but that doesn't mean that the weather is somehow free of the laws of physics to act on its own. To believe that choice is absolutely free of determining factors is to harbor the absurd belief that the chooser is beyond the control of cosmic laws.

The belief that nothing can escape the laws of science requires rejecting the notion of free will. All the causes for making one choice over another are far too numerous and complex to identify, but that doesn't mean that they don't exist. Human lives are molded and formed by the same laws of science that govern the growth of trees, the behavior of dogs, and the formation and destruction of mountains. The ignorance of the infinitely complex web of cause and effect creates the illusion of free choice.

Much time and effort is required to search for causes. Casting blame and attributing misbehavior to simply making the wrong choices not only takes little effort but is emotionally satisfying, eliciting feelings of superiority for taking the moral high ground by freely choosing the right path. It's so much easier for the insecure teacher or parent to tell little Johnny, "You're a big boy, you're five years old, you know how to behave, why can't you be good like your sister?" Depending on the act or how often Johnny gets in trouble, the believer in free will may denounce the boy as a hopelessly bad child deserving of harsh punishment to straighten him out. The teacher who subscribes to determinism, objective and secure in her own identity, may still temporarily isolate Johnny from the class but will not be so condemnatory and judgmental. In her more determined search for causes, she may discover that the child got to bed late, had no breakfast, has a learning difficulty, and comes from a broken home.

The determinist is more likely to search for causes and solutions. If I believe actions and beliefs are caused by many factors other than just free choice, then I am more likely to empathize with you as an equal being. I am better able to dismantle hate and encourage love by searching for causes. The humility that stems from believing in interconnectedness calms anger and reduces impatience when the universe doesn't obey our commands and when people fail to meet our expectations.

It makes no more sense to condemn my neighbor for playing music too loud than it does to harbor a grudge against the heavens for allowing thunder and lightning to interrupt my sleep. Both are situations that must be dealt with, and both are situations that have many causes. That the elements don't have free will doesn't prevent me from using an umbrella, nor does the fact that my neighbors don't have free will prevent me from confronting them about the loud music, but it does allow for a reasonable and unemotional search for solutions. A justice system that recognizes a deterministic world will still have prisons and may permanently confine incorrigibles, but it will also treat criminals more humanely.

Isolating cause and effect simplifies life. Looking for multiple causes is contrary to the way a dualistic brain works. It is easy and emotionally satisfying to place the blame for a loss on the kicker for missing a field goal in the last seconds of the game, but ignored are the countless factors that contributed to the outcome, such as injuries to inspirational players, missed blocks and tackles, and careless penalties in addition to coaching errors. The search for the single cause, like the belief in free will, is the easy way out. The objective determinist will see the universe as a unified web of interrelated causes and effects.

What is even more absurd is the Christian belief that God will render eternal punishment to those who either make wrong choices or who fail to repent for their misdeeds. This belief means that a so-called loving, forgiving, and all-knowing God made humankind in its image, created some people knowing ahead of time that they would be unbelievers, and then set them up by sending them to hell for their pagan beliefs. On the other hand, if God doesn't know human destiny, then it loses its all-powerful, omniscient nature.

One might think that if there is no free will, if we are not masters of our own fate, then what is the point of trying to improve our lives or do much of anything? Why punish criminals if they are only victims of fate? This is not my position at all. Determinism is not fatalism, and people can still be held accountable for making wrong choices. When I encouraged my sons to do well in school, the positive reinforcement became one of many important determining influences in their lives, and assigning them a time-out for misbehavior helped encourage them to improve their behavior. My sons' behaviors have causes and whether I encourage them or not is one cause in an infinite chain of cause and effect. In a deterministic society criminal behavior is still dealt with. Just as a determinist repairs a broken fence, so does the determinist deal with "broken" behavior. The believer in free will may criticize a smoker for continuing such a stupid habit and wonder why the smoker doesn't simply choose to stop. As a determinist, I am more aware that the choice to smoke or quit doesn't just come out of thin air, but is due to a host of causes. I can actually be one of the external factors that may encourage the smoker to quit.

Even the most die-hard free-will advocate will admit that actions to some extent are influenced by certain environmental and hereditary factors. It is generally agreed that heredity, education, parental upbringing, friends, and relationships, and many other factors, are important determinants in life. The question is how much influence do these factors have? The notion that one can be just a little bit free is like saying that a woman can be just a little bit pregnant. It is my contention that if all the genetic and environmental conditions were known, it would be obvious that free will is an illusion.

Perhaps some will argue that the latest revelations of quantum mechanics brings an element of indeterminism into the mix, but the quantum world operates on the subatomic level, not in the large-scale world of human activity where cause and effect rule. Quantum fluctuations and indeterminacy may cause the assassin's finger to exert more or less pressure on the trigger than intended, but it won't influence the decision to shoot.

By denying free will, it might seem that I am contradicting myself since I have previously stated the importance of utilizing the power of creation to freely choose to see the beauty in the marvelous mundane and to create meaning where before none existed. Humans do have this power of creation, but innumerable factors, including possibly this book, determine how the creative faculty is put to use.

It is autumn as I write these words, and as I look out the window I see leaves from our liquid amber tree floating to the ground. Suppose these leaves become conscious and one arrogant leaf that has fallen a fraction of a second later than the others looks with contempt at the inferior leaf whose position and rate of descent puts it a little closer to the ground. And the leaf that is closest to the ground looks with equal contempt at the leaves already on the ground. Another leaf, still attached to the tree, feels superior to all the leaves, and all of these leaves, unaware as they are of their own nature and of the influence of the seasons and weather, would think they are fully in control of their destiny. In a way, humans are as absurd as these leaves since they also rank their standing based on their position in the fall.

For a while the green leaves flourish while still attached to the Tree of Life. Then they fall, and they fall at slightly different speeds, in slightly different places, but they all end up on the ground. The tree looks at its leaves in an entirely different way from how the leaves look at themselves. Mother tree depends on dead and decayed leaves to provide its roots with nutrients for growth and survival. The fallen leaves become just as important to the tree as the leaves that are still attached.

Like the leaves on a tree, each individual struggles mightily to remain attached to the Tree of Life. However, humans judge the worth of the attachment and the fall. Because of different circumstances, everyone falls at different rates, in different ways, but eventually all will fall. The dead leaves turn to mulch that enriches and nourishes the soil so that the tree can go on living. No human is better or worse than any other human. Just different.

Passing through life, we are like the lonely falling leaf, filled with the anxiety of separation, fearfully dreading the crash to the ground, unaware of the conditions governing the fall. Awareness only of separation creates the illusion of standing alone with the power of free will. Awareness and understanding of the determinants of our thoughts and actions lead to true freedom.

Knowing the true cause of actions and beliefs brings freedom from prideful notions for which undue credit or blame is taken. A unique set of DNA, upbringing, and circumstance determines what we are, and for this neither blame nor credit can be assigned. In my days as a teacher I would occasionally challenge the Board of Education at public meetings, an act that several teachers said required a great deal of courage. My response was that it would take more courage for me to keep my mouth shut, that it was simply my nature to speak out, and that there were possibly other life situations for which I might be accused of cowardice.

Like the leaf struggling to stay on the tree, we think control and position are everything. We look for the right friends, the right job, the right place to live, the right beliefs, the right spouse, all in a vain search for that one utopian position, that missing piece, where Perfection is located. Now, there is nothing wrong with this search; in fact, control is a huge concern of humankind. We like to think destiny is ours to control, yet the natural laws and workings of the universe determine our lives just as certainly as they do the lives of all other creatures.

Think for a moment of the ridiculous cosmology that free will demands. Imagine that the Great Cosmo is looking at the unfolding of the universe after the Big Bang. It sees all the stuff of the universe being hurled about in all directions, and this stuff of course is under the control of Cosmo's laws. But on one small speck of a planet a few tiny life forms seem to be under the influence of a strange ego force that gives them the illusion of being gods in control of their own private realm. These humans are deluded into arrogantly thinking that they possess the special power to make decisions completely free of the forces that govern the rest of the universe.

Maximizing Freedom

Although the laws of nature can't be escaped, the sense of freedom can be maximized by living in harmony with the order of Cosmo. Life-satisfaction and freedom increase with the understanding of how the principles of cosmic order apply to everyday living. For instance, if I try to win friends by deceit and selfish actions, I am asking for trouble, since I have failed to connect Newton's physical law—for every action there is an opposite reaction—with the Golden Rule, which is its spiritual corollary. An unbalanced life characterized by extremes may suffer from addictions and various mental illnesses as a consequence of ignoring Cosmo's principle of balance and symmetry. It is from the centered Self that one finds the maximum freedom from extremes.

Happiness and well-being reward a life aligned with the truth of connections, while misery and alienation are the consequences of separation and isolation. Married couples, people with extensive social contacts, and those who reach out to others live longer and healthier lives. A life emphasizing separation and differences rather than similarities and connections becomes fragmented in a futile fight against the grain of evolution and cosmic order.

Everything is part of the natural order, but the more advanced the civilization, the more humankind becomes separated from nature by trying to create its own order. Human potential is realized and civilization benefits when the order of humanity and the order of nature are in harmony. I grow closer to Cosmo by humbly accepting my connection to the same forces that shape and mold the cosmos. And it is by means of this acceptance that I connect with the divine present that is the I Am that I seek.

CHAPTER 12

FINDING ENLIGHTENMENT

The Jesus Commandment

I have previously referred to what I call the Jesus Commandment, more commonly called the Great Commandment, but these profound words, whether or not they were actually stated by Jesus, pretty well sum up what makes the good life. When he was asked by a lawyer which is the greatest commandment that offers eternal life, Jesus replied, "Love God with all your heart, and with all your soul, and with all your strength, and with all of your mind, and your neighbor as yourself. Do this and you will live. On these commandments depend all the law and the prophets" (Luke 10:25-28, Matthew 22:36-40).

What is somewhat unusual about this Jesus Commandment is the mention of self-love. Self-love often has a negative connotation. However, the other can't be loved without loving the Self since, in essence, we are all different manifestations or expressions of the Great Cosmo, for as expressed in the Tao, "Thou art that." When I love my true Self, my core being, I am connecting with a Self that is common to all. The uniting of the spiritual and physical is perfected as each partner opens to the perfection of Self. At the moment self-love is attained we become open to the perfection of the other. By valuing my own existence, I lose ego attachment, defensive barriers break down, and, with open arms and great confidence, I accept you into my world. And it will not be just you that is accepted, but my self-love will allow me to see my connection with all the various forms of the other. For this reason, Jesus instructs us to love the Self, knowing that connecting with the divine within will be followed by love for others. It actually makes no difference which aspect of this Trinity (God, Self, Other) is loved first, for if one aspect is loved, then all are loved, since in actuality, the God, Self, and Other are equal and interdependent.

Man and woman must first be human before they can be divine; they must love Self before they can love God, but the devil and the divine both partake in human nature. Man and woman are really God in disguise, hiding from itself. Recognize "the mystery hidden for ages is Christ in you" (Col. 1:27) and have faith that when the false self is left behind, "I live, yet no longer I but Christ lives in me" (Gal. 2:20). Total acceptance and love of Self naturally involves total acceptance and love of God and other.

Start with loving the subjective I Am. Just count to one, since loving one is the same as loving all. This is the Equality of Selves. One is the identity number. One multiplied by itself is one, one divided by one is still one. By uniting with the other, we begin to see the other in us and may even sense that the other is us. But the obvious place to start is by loving the authentic and divine Self within.

There are many deeply ingrained attitudes that oppose thinking too highly of oneself. It is wrongly taught that loving the Self is a sign of vanity and egotism, and that love for Self precludes love for other. This is only true if Self is identified with Positions and Possessions. Our hang-up is the false belief that accepting the Self necessitates rejecting the other, or accepting the other means rejecting the Self. The teaching should be exactly the opposite—the secret to loving the other is to love the authentic Self. Only if you are confident of who you are can you reach out to the other. By accepting the Equality of Selves, loving Self is loving other. Now the two become one, and the puzzle is finally complete.

It is a common notion that the Self is incomplete, that somehow an important piece or connection is missing. People have been taught and conditioned to believe that God, or perfection, is out there, separate from us, that we can't be the whole truth, but only a small part of it, because only God is complete. The misconception is that to be worthy of love requires being so much more than what one already is.

Doubts about personal value may be the biggest stumbling block to self-love, and of course also to loving the other. We doubt our knowledge, moral character, physical appearance, and we certainly doubt our divinity. We are lazy and ignorant, we procrastinate, we have nasty habits, sometimes we are cruel and thoughtless; how can such an inferior person, riddled with so many weaknesses and defects, be worthy of anyone's love? We generalize by thinking that all of these traits are locked into the Self. It doesn't help that Christians preach that man is born in sin.

It just seems like there is so much room for improvement and that in so many ways humans fall short of the ideal. But the problem is the tendency to focus on the lack of some quality, such as generosity or love, as if these are separate entities to be worked on. All aspects of personality are interrelated, and it all has to do with establishing connections with others. By understanding that truth of other is truth of Self, one finds that all the positive traits of being human automatically become incorporated into Self. Remember, to understand is to love. The most important understanding is that truth of Self is truth of other.

Don't get me wrong. I am not saying that we shouldn't strive to be better. But any so-called personal failings are not part of the perfection of the always present but often hidden authentic Self that is our centered creative power. There is the tendency to dwell on past mistakes, and to magnify them way out of proportion.

Our attitude toward time seriously impedes our realization of the human potential for love of Self, God and other. The desire for the eternal and the absolute, and the related belief that more is merrier and bigger is better, strongly influences attitudes toward time. It's common sense that a longer time period is desirable for many things such as long-lasting lipstick, long-lasting tires, and a long-lasting life. However, time duration is irrelevant as it relates to the authentic Self, just as time is irrelevant as it relates to truth.

Length of time and size or quantity have nothing to do with the authentic Self, or with experiencing self-transcendent emotions, or with the experience of enlightenment. It is unnecessary to be permanently humble; there are no time requirements for good behavior. No matter how cruel or indifferent I was last week, or yesterday, or ten minutes ago, if I am not only empathetic now, but if, from the detached centered position of the Self, I recognize the inauthenticity of the former and deeply live the truth of the latter, then I am on the right path.

There is no time like the present. The fact that people believed the earth was flat for a longer period of time than we've known it to be round does not make the present truth any less true. There is no time limit to truth. The truth, like the present moment, is eternally true, whether we're aware of it or not.

Truth is unrelated to concepts of size or quantity though we berate ourselves unmercifully for what we judge to be the number and severity of past sins. Any brief, but deeply experienced encounter with truth, is a moment of enlightenment, a moment to celebrate, a moment of satori. And these moments will flash on and off for this is the nature of existence.

Quantity is irrelevant to authenticity. Since quantity is an attribute associated with the world of space-time-matter, it is unnecessary to accumulate virtue points by piling up virtuous acts to counter the seven sins. Virtue is its own reward, but only true connection with the virtue of love is necessary, and love stems from understanding. For just as connecting with Self is connecting with Cosmo and other, so other virtues will be encompassed if love permeates one's being.

Certain troubling questions arise from what I have said about unconditional self-acceptance. Does this mean that a murderer should feel no remorse? Wouldn't unconditional self-acceptance grant permission to commit any number of unethical or criminal offenses against others? Where would the motivation be for self-improvement? The answer to these troubling questions is that loving the Self requires the conscious realization of an intimate interrelationship with the other, which allows the Self to see its reflection in the other. To understand (to love) the Self is to understand the Great Cosmo, and to realize that an offense to Self is an offense against you, as well as an offense to the truth of Cosmo. Acceptance of the true value of Self and other happen together.

The Golden Rule

Doing unto others as you would have them do unto you—this is not only the foundation for morality but is the way to realizing the cosmic purpose to resolving the polarity between Self and other.

When Confucius was asked by his disciples which of his teachings was most important, he answered, "Never do to others what you would not have them do to you." The Golden Rule, stated in negative terms in Buddhism and Hinduism, was stated positively as a spiritual principle that Jesus put on the same plane with loving God, Self, and other. In Matthew 7:12 he said, "So whatever you wish that men would do to you, do so to them; for this sums up the law and the prophets."

The application of the Golden Rule requires people to step outside the false self to be in the place of the other by understanding the Truth of Selves, the equality of all. The Buddhist, Confucian, and Hindu way is to always be aware of what causes you suffering and then seek to avoid inflicting that pain on others. The Christian approach, more active and extroverted, is to be aware of what makes you feel good, and then seek to bring the same joy and pleasure to others. The practice of the Golden Rule fosters compassion.

The Wisdom of Old Age

"Wow, you look great!" At my age, when people tell me this it really means, "Hey, I can't believe you're still standing upright."

Americans live in a world shaped by the values of youth. Civilization certainly needs youthful passion and energy, but not to the exclusion of the wisdom of age. With the keepers of wisdom penned up in nursing facilities and retirement centers, we are left with impatient youth immersed in material identities, ruled by passions, and absorbed in concerns of the ego.

The youthful desires for excitement and stimulation impede the understanding of life's lessons. On the surface it would appear that young people are totally involved in the moment—so much so, however, that others are often neglected—as well as the practical necessity of planning for the future. The present moment for young people is dominated by concerns with appearances, stylish clothes, fast cars, and a desperate grab for experiences that provide the maximum in sensory stimulation. Now, of course I am exaggerating a little to make a point. Many young people do have a deep appreciation for nature and the solitary pleasure of a walk in the park. However, what the culture of youth often lacks is appreciation and awareness of relationships and connections with the larger picture.

Declining senses mean less importance is placed on appearances. Advancing age provides the opportunity to experience a reality beyond appearances and material, a reality that offers greater meaning and contentment than is found in the turmoil of youth. The acute sensory system of the young can lead to judgmental attitudes capable of spotting every defect and spot of dust. With advanced age, things begin to slip and sag, control is diminished, tension and conflict begin to slip away in quiet submission to the forces that be, and, with my poor vision, I can no longer spot that little speck of dust on your piano.

Yes, the aging body loses definition, and the world itself becomes less distinct as sensory apparatus begins to fail. But as physical boundaries blur, psychological and social barriers begin to fall. As judgments and criticisms lesson, separation fades, allowing a vision of a greater unified picture to emerge. As definition and separation lose importance, unity and connectedness take on added meaning, more value is placed on friends and family and isn't this what we have been seeking all along? Losing the ability to precisely measure and compare causes us to also lose the sense of position, so I no longer care so much about which side I am on. I lose the constant inner turmoil caused by the attempt to deal with polarities.

Age fosters an awareness of a boundless authentic Self that doesn't depend on seeing or hearing, or even conceptualizing. The quiet, inner world of the elderly is a place of unity and interconnections where gratitude is shown for the value of the other, whether the other takes the form of a simple meal, a stormy day, or a friend. As senses become less acute, as mobility and physical freedom are lost, as friends die and health declines, the power of creation remains, which permits me to choose the higher value and to perhaps be grateful for the simple process of being.

Strength, speed, and location assume less importance as physical mobility declines. Priorities change, attitudes change. Envy, impatience, and prideful identities formerly based on Possessions and Positions are replaced with patience, humility, empathy, and an openness to the other. Pleasure is found in the marvelous mundane—the bird on the windowsill, the neighbor's beautiful flowers, the ever-changing cloud formations.

As attachments fade, the inner light shines, and, step by step, we learn nature's lesson that to lose is to gain. We finally see that from the state of nothingness arises the power to create all meaning. Ah, what a wonderful feeling of relief and freedom is gained from downsizing the house and discovering the truth that the reward is in the giving.

But let's not kid ourselves; obviously there is a downside to physical decline, the many aches and pains are tough to deal with. The challenge as we age and mature is to learn the lessons before the decline becomes too great. In fact, as alluded to earlier, the lessons of life can be learned at many levels. One doesn't have to be deaf to appreciate silence, or blind to see that beauty goes beyond the physical, nor does one have to be a centenarian to gain the wisdom of age.

As victims of a youth-dominated society, the elderly remain trapped in a material world that values sharp definition and separation. Naturally, as many oldsters fumble and stumble, blind as a bat and deaf as a stump, they may not see anything desirable about dimmed eyesight and poor hearing. The fight against nature begins with the appearance of the first wrinkle or wisp of gray hair. Entropy and the force of gravity is fought in every possible way with eyeglasses, hearing aids, dyed hair, and hair transplants. Everything that gravity drags down we try to raise back up with facelifts, breast lifts, and butt lifts.

Nature has a reason for blurring distinctions and definitions. The party can't last forever, and if it did, it would be about as boring as a song would be if a favorite line was played over and over. Deadlines not only spur us on to clean and straighten up in preparation for an up-coming event but to also have a better time once the party begins. As material creatures, we naturally value the time when material appears sharp and distinct. But this is only one act in life's play. Happiness and meaning aren't found in only one act. Life, like existence itself, is a continual cyclical process, and happiness depends on successfully playing the game of Catch and Release. The continual challenge of life is figuring out when to release attachment and move on to the next act. Is Cosmo preparing us for entry into a material-free reality?

The experience of aging and the decline of the physical can teach many lessons. The loss of eyesight reveals that insight is more profound than out-sight. Conversation, as it becomes more difficult to hear, takes on new meaning with the realization that much talking is rife with idle prattle meant to fill moments of awkward silence, or relates to seeking reaffirmation for personal beliefs and one's own worth. Even the loss of hearing can be a blessing as one learns to enjoy the sound of silence. But with age, not just physical noise lessens; the noise of the ego softens. What remains acute is the most important sense of all, the sense of wonder and gratitude for the presence of the other in all its forms.

With old age, death rears its head. Death is the absolute limit that gives life meaning. Following the law of supply and demand, as our remaining time on earth grows short, the value of the moment increases, as well as the value of what the moment contains. However, the fully lived moment is absent the fear of death.

With the end time growing near, we find that time, the vessel of life, assumes importance in itself. No longer is there the desperate need to fill time in order to become unaware of time's passing. Regardless of what one has done, or where one has been, experiences vanish in the wind. Existence and awareness of existence assume more value. The one permanence is awareness of present being, the I Am.

Consciousness evolves as the body devolves, providing one has learned the lessons of the physical. But time is irrelevant to enlightened knowledge of the authentic Self. The Hermetic maxim, "As above, so below, as below, so above," unlocks the profound truth that it is unnecessary to personally experience old age in order to learn the lessons of aging—every moment and every place contains the truth we seek.

When we die we are still with Cosmo. The universe has played Catch with us for a while. It threw us the ball, and in so doing, potential energy manifested itself in material form. But eventually the ball must be released. When material becomes disorganized we return to God. Human progresses to God, God progresses to human, and the cycle continues.

CHAPTER 13

CONCLUSION

We may imagine enlightenment as floating blissfully in a cloud of constant joy and contentment, free of problems and worries. There are a few good actors around. A fortunate few are blessed with a genetic make-up and life circumstances that predispose them to naturally having fantastic personalities bubbling over with love, patience, intelligence, humor, and all the good traits. The reality of being trapped in a universe of separation and material form is that discontent and loneliness inevitably arise as will conflict and opposition.

The human experience necessarily involves suffering the anxiety of the illusion of separation from the infinite. However, admittedly without any empirical evidence, I believe that permeating all the layers of the human brain, from the reptilian basal ganglia to the conceptualizing cerebral cortex, is the driving force of the Will to Unify that arises out of this deficiency, out of the desire for absolute connection. This driving force may be the cosmic impetus for material to reunite as a singularity of pure energy, the drive that underlies the universal need for religion that seeks to overcome the anxiety of death and separation.

However, the gift of creation can soften harsh realities by finding moments of oneness and flow that permit one to step outside the restrictive boundaries of convention and Identifictions, to transcend and transform the mundane everyday world into an experience of awesome joy and wonder.

There are no techniques to follow and no harsh discipline required; in fact, it is just the opposite. Burdened with attachment to the desire for enlightenment, seekers often dissect the process of The Way into so many bits and pieces that the experience is lost. Relax! Let go. If you are open to your inner perfection, love of Self and other will be yours. Let down defensive boundaries, let the other in. Seek to understand the other, see yourself in the other, see the value of the other, see how cycles, contrast and the struggle to resolve the polarity of separation and unity fit into both of your lives, as does an appreciation of form and symmetry.

Life is a metaphor for the Order of Cosmo. Know the nature of existence and you know the essence of Self. Cosmo's ground of being is my ground of being, the essence of Cosmo the Creator is my essence. And what is that essence? The infinite potential of a dynamic, creative mind.

We think we would be satisfied with our lives if only we could somehow leave a lasting impression, like the superhero who saves the human race. Well, our life involves more than helping humankind. By understanding and realizing the enlightened Self, we are consciously participating in Cosmo's continuing evolution toward a state of unity. Realizing human potential depends on self-acceptance, which is fulfilled by reaching out to other, knowing how Self is other. By experiencing our worth as being equal to the worth of the other, by loving Neighbor and God as Self, we exercise humankind's divine gift: the ability to see the connection between God and human, between Self and other.

Seeing and living the connection between Self and other makes clear that the process of Self is the same as the process of the divine. Live and think the connections. Love of Self is incomplete without love of nature, see the connection, see Self in other.

Humankind, like the cosmos, consists of interconnected levels of organization, each with its own established boundaries, yet also sharing the boundaries of the other. Living cells are unique and separate, as is the body, yet a part of each is included in the other. Subatomic particles are unique and separate, as are molecules and compounds, yet each of these is also a part of the other. All of these constituent parts are included in the infinite mind of Cosmo.

The individual is separate yet possessing the potential to realize its link with all levels—self, community, nation, humankind, planet, and cosmos. The challenge is to recognize, value, understand, be grateful for and hence love the other while still remaining a separate Self. The flourishing of humankind and the cosmos depend on the flow of positive information between these levels.

Understand your connection and role as an integrated piece of the puzzle, or pixel of the picture. When considering new legislation, a politician doesn't just represent an isolated district but also must think of the legislation's impact on the nation and the world. Labor unions can't just demand higher and higher pensions and health plans without considering how the cost of benefits impacts the corporation. Nations, corporations, and individuals must be aware that pollution travels worldwide.

Quality of life increases with the understanding and appreciation of how humans interconnect with different levels of organization. Countless research studies discuss how positive physical and mental connections increase mental and physical well-being by releasing beneficial neurotransmitters and hormones.

Being centered allows for the connection with different levels of organization. From the center one is free to look in all directions, inside and out, up and down, near and far.

Don't make things such a big deal. Eons ago, human survival depended on making a big deal out of everything, especially the Super Me's own sense of self-importance. True, we are still a supremely important big deal, but then so is everyone else. Finding acceptance, value and significance requires accepting the significant value of the other.

Polarity and duality are facts of existence, or at least of existence as known by humans. Everything comes in pairs—life and death, male and female, subject and object, positive and negative. Our discontent is the conscious experience of nature's continual conflict with duality, life and death being the ultimate duality. Although death gives birth to life, life resists death with all its might. Just as existence implies nonexistence, I am implies I am not; one side of the equation requires the other. Part of who I am is who I am not and all that I reject. Enlightened unity consciousness is found to the extent that we recognize and deal with the dark side and use its power to augment the divine in the same way that the sun's hellish nuclear inferno is essential to life on earth. Be mindful that stress is not the problem; it is how stress is viewed that counts.

Notice what is around you, feel what is around you, and then step back, release, laugh and play the game seriously in good humor. Feel the transcendent emotions of wonder, awe and gratitude that take you beyond the Self to connect with other. Use your creative power to attribute positive value. Don't take so much for granted. Be grateful. Enjoy the warmth of the sun and the friendship of others. Smell the rose, inhale the fragrance, enjoy and marvel at its spiraling symmetry. This game of life is over in a cosmic blink, so enjoy it, don't take it for granted, be grateful and show gratitude. Be aware of the game and play it seriously in good humor.

Always a little behind or a little ahead, the present is often passed by. In reality, we exist as a field-of-being that fits into a web of interrelated aspects, a continuum ranging like the Taoist symbol of the yin-yang, each of this contains a little bit of that. In an instant, the present is both the past and the future. It is the entire picture that is important, not just one pole or the other, subject or object, or this time or that place. In the cyclical universe there really are no ends, for what appear to be ends are only the beginnings of other cycles of the continuing process.

Everything is perfect because Cosmo's laws work perfectly. Everything happens just the way it is supposed to. There are not some parts of the universe more perfect than other parts. You already are the perfect answer, the subject of your search. What we really want is what we already are but don't see and don't believe. That being said, the perfect laws can still make a lousy cup of coffee. With a little help, I know that barista can do better.

AFTERWORD

Frantically, I raced down twisting city streets to elude the pursuers in their super-charged muscle car. At a dead-end, I escaped onto abandoned railroad tracks, which dumped me into an open field where the car immediately bogged down in sand. Desperately, I gunned the engine, to no avail. The pursuers screeched to a halt right behind me. Shaking with fear, certain they'd beat me or worse, I exited the disabled vehicle and surrendered to two menacing, hulking men attired in odd costumes, their faces and bodies strangely adorned with garish paint.

Without speaking, one man gestured for me to sit across from them at a table where his partner sat mixing a concoction of paint to apply to my body. Sitting opposite the paint-mixer, still terrified, I caught his gaze. Ignoring his dreadful appearance, I stared directly into his eyes. I sensed his fear, loneliness and vulnerability—it seemed to mirror my own. I hoped by somehow touching his human spirit he might show compassion and mercy. I asked his name. Without hesitation, he gave me a strange name that I can't remember.

Suddenly, a wave of relief overcame my dread and fear. I asked the other man his name. He responded but no other words were spoken. I now felt assured they meant no harm but only intended to paint me to look like them. I felt compassion, not only for my abductors, but for my own fearful self that lay hidden beneath the facade of conventionality. Now all of us relaxed.

I laughed, a hearty, tension-relieving laugh at the absurdity of the web of delusions of my own making that disguise the authentic self.

And at that exact moment, at 1:01 am, I woke up from my

dream. My sister, Carol, her body ravaged by cancer, had died ten hours earlier. The time, 1:01, was a vivid reminder of an essay Carol wrote two weeks earlier entitled "Connections," and of a related discussion of how negotiating the choices and polarities of life is like the off-on, zero-one binary language of computers.

The dream brought home to me that navigating life's fears and loneliness, and the search for authenticity and meaning, require leaving the familiar tracks of convention and conformity. Forming connections with the other—sometimes one's own self—requires exiting the vehicle that shelters the disguised self.

This dream, and the end-of-life discussions with Carol, inspired me to write this book. The countless bull sessions over many years that I've had with my life-long friend, Steve Ruckman, led to many of the insights I've recorded.

Acknowledgement

My immense gratitude to Stephen Ruckman, a long-time friend, for the many late night philosophical conversations and for his amazing patience in listening to my long-winded monologues. Special thanks to Professor Peter Koestenbaum, recipient of the California Outstanding Professor award, whose unique approach to Existentialism has been essential to much of my thinking. Thanks to my first editor, Jessica Vineyard. Thanks to Wes Fornes, to my wife Arlene, my son Daniel, to my friends Dr. Louis Segesvary and William O'Haren, and to my sister, Joan Carter, for their valuable suggestions or help in editing. A special thanks to John Dorrance for helping me select a title. Thanks to Steve Behaerman, the cosmic comic who is also known as Swami Beyondananda, for showing me how the spiritual journey involves humor. Special thanks to my very patient and generous publisher, Keith Swenson at Purple Hills Books.

ABOUT THE AUTHOR

The author, a native Californian, has lived most of his life in Silicon Valley where he taught science for many years. Upon retiring, Tom came to the realization that since many of the books on philosophy were essentially stating the same truths from different perspectives, he could advance his own understanding and conscious evolution only by writing the truth from his perspective. In addition to pursuing his life-long interest in philosophy and metaphysics, Tom travels the world as an amateur photographer. He now resides in San Jose with his wife, who is also a retired educator. They have two grown sons.

DARWIN'S APPLE
The Evolutionary
Biology of Religion
Mitchell Diamond

INDEX

CPSIA information can be obtained
at www.ICGtesting.com
Printed in the USA
LVHW052146190219
608120LV00037B/792/P